1985

Religion and State in the Kingdom of Saudi Arabia

Also of Interest

†*Islam: Continuity and Change in the Modern World,* John Obert Voll

†*Religion and Politics in the Middle East,* edited by Michael Curtis

†*A Concise History of the Middle East,* Second Edition, Revised and Updated, Arthur Goldschmidt, Jr.

†*Political Behavior in the Arab States,* edited by Tawfic E. Farah

†*The Foreign Policies of Arab States,* edited by Bahgat Korany and Ali E. Hillal Dessouki

The Problems of Arab Economic Development and Integration, edited by Adda Guecioueur

The Gulf and the Search for Strategic Stability: Saudi Arabia, the Military Balance in the Gulf, and Trends in the Arab-Israeli Military Balance, Anthony H. Cordesman

†Available in hardcover and paperback.

Westview Special Studies on the Middle East

Religion and State in the Kingdom of Saudi Arabia
Ayman Al-Yassini

Perhaps more than any other country, Saudi Arabia is identified with Islam. It is the center of Muslim prayers and pilgrimages; the *Quran* is its constitution and the *shari'ah* the source of its laws; legitimacy of the House of Saud is based on a combination of religious and tribal-dynastic factors. Since the discovery of oil in Saudi Arabia in the 1930s, as modernization began to take place in the areas of industry, education, communications, bureaucracy, and administration, the political elite has sought to maintain traditional values while developing materially. Dr. Al-Yassini examines the complex processes by which the traditional relationships between religion, society, and polity are being radically altered in the modern Saudi state. His study focuses on these critical questions: Will the differentiation between religion and state increase? Or will a modus vivendi and mutual accommodation between the two be worked out, whereby the state will slow the process of modernization and the religious elite will accept some elements of change?

Dr. Ayman Al-Yassini is director of Public Affairs at the Canadian Bureau for International Education. He was formerly a staff fellow in political science at the Centre for Developing-Area Studies at McGill University and visiting lecturer in the university's Department of Political Science. Dr. Al-Yassini's recent publications include *Religion and Foreign Policy in Saudi Arabia* (1983).

To my parents,
Soubhi and Wafika,
for their support and love

Religion and State in the Kingdom of Saudi Arabia

Ayman Al-Yassini

Westview Press / Boulder and London

Westview Special Studies on the Middle East

Copyright © 1985 by Westview Press, Inc.

Published in 1985 in the United States of America by Westview Press, Inc., 5500 Central Avenue, Boulder, Colorado 80301; Frederick A. Praeger, Publisher

Library of Congress Cataloging in Publication Data
Al-Yassini, Ayman.
  Religion and state in the kingdom of Saudi Arabia.
  (Westview special studies on the Middle East)
  Bibliography: p.
  Includes index.
  1. Islam and state—Saudi Arabia. 2. Saudi Arabia—
Politics and government. I. Title. II. Series.
BP63.S33A48 1985   322'.1'09538   84-13043
ISBN 0-8133-0058-4

Printed and bound in the United States of America

10   9   8   7   6   5   4   3   2   1

Contents

vii

Tables

Preface

This study deals with the relationship between religion and state in the Kingdom of Saudi Arabia. More than any other country in the Muslim world, Saudi Arabia is identified with Islam. Home of Mecca and Medina, the center of Muslim prayers and pilgrimage, the kingdom's religious character was reconfirmed in 1745 when Shaykh Muhammad Ibn Abd al-Wahhab allied himself with Al Saud, rulers of Dar'iya in central Najd. This alliance continues today. Islam is the state religion, the source of political legitimacy; it shapes state policies and activities and serves as the moral code of society. Because of its Wahhabi character, the kingdom is viewed by many Muslims as fundamentalist.

The findings of this study indicate that despite its fundamentalist ideology, the Saudi kingdom is becoming secular. The state expanded its jurisdiction to many areas that were formerly regulated by religion and the religious establishment. The ulama became incorporated in state administration, and state laws regulate ulama activities. The state, because of its monopoly of power and resources and its need to maintain autonomy, does not tolerate an autonomous religious domain that may compete with it for the loyalty of citizens. Thus the state extended its jurisdiction to the religious domain and utilized religious leaders to legitimate its policies.

My interest in the relationship between religion and state was inspired by my reading of Thomas Bruneau's book, *The Political Transformation of the Brazilian Catholic Church* (London: Cambridge University Press, 1974). My gratitude to Thomas Bruneau, who acted as my academic adviser and as director of research at McGill University, is of a kind that can hardly be expressed adequately in the form of an acknowledgment. To Charles Adams of the Institute of Islamic Studies, McGill University, I owe a special debt of appreciation for assisting me at various stages of research with advice and interest in the project. I also thank André Dirlik of the Royal Military College at St. Jean, Quebec, for commenting on an earlier draft of this study.

Research for the study was undertaken in Riyadh, Saudi Arabia from 1979 to 1980. Thanks are due to a large number of Saudis and Saudi institutions who assisted my project. First, my colleagues at Riyadh University, College of Administrative Sciences, Drs. Omar al-Amoudi, Abd Allah al-Qaba', and Abd al-Ghader Abd al-Ghafar, provided moral support, read the outline, and suggested modification. Second, the following institutions provided information and assistance: ARAMCO; the Saudi ministries of Information, Finance, and Planning; the World Association of Muslim Youth; the Directorate of Ifta', Da'wa, and Guidance; the Committees for Commanding the Good and Forbidding Evil; and Darat al-Malik Abd al-Aziz (research center).

The actual writing of the study was completed between 1980 and 1982 at the Centre for Developing-Area Studies at McGill University. My affiliation with the Centre since 1974 as a research fellow, its excellent research facilities, and the intellectual stimulation provided by my colleagues there are all most appreciated. To the Centre's former director and associate director, Drs. Thomas C. Bruneau and Thomas Eisemon, respectively, my thanks for their support. To the present director, Dr. Warwick Armstrong, my appreciation for his continued interest in my research projects. To my friend, Dr. Kevin Tun-teng, Vanier College, thanks for assisting me in editing the manuscript. To Dr. Baha Abu Laban, vice-president for research at the University of Alberta, my appreciation for his contributions to and interest in my research.

Finally, I am forever grateful for the patient endurance, the understanding, and the many gestures of encouragement from my wife, Colette, and my son, Sammy. They made life in Saudi Arabia more pleasant.

A Note on Transliteration

In this study, I have used the spelling most commonly accepted in the literature on Saudi Arabia—for example, Riyadh, Jeddah, Ibn Saud, and Medina.

Ayman Al-Yassini

Part 1

Religion and State in Islam

Introduction

The theory of the Islamic polity in its classical form did not envision the separation of religion and politics. Since Islam had no hierarchical religious institutions analogous to the organization of the Christian church, the historical experience of Muslims shows the concentration of authority in the hands of temporal power. The caliph was Prince of the Faithful as well as successor to the Prophet. He was entrusted with the administration of justice and the implementation of the dictates of the *shari'ah* (Islamic law). Religious scholars, however, began to remove themselves from state authority in order to maintain a measure of autonomy. This was brought about by two developments: (1) the gradual transfer of power positions to non-Arab elements, such as Persians, Turks, and Mongols, during Abbasid rule; and (2) the general decline that befell the Muslim state. Alarmed by these developments and fearing the effect on their discipline and status, the ulama (religious leaders) set themselves as the guardians and sole interpreters of the *shari'ah*.

In more recent times, Muslim societies have had to face new realities. The disintegration of the Ottoman empire following World War I resulted in the loss of the major political entity that had provided a semblance of unity. Later on, Muslim societies encountered a more dynamic Western civilization, which threatened their survival. Consequently, Muslims were pushed to establish modern states of their own in order to maintain their identity. In the process, they raised the following question: What changes should be introduced into the relationship between religion and state in order to accommodate the new realities? The subsequent experience of the Muslim states suggests that the current relationship between religion and state conforms to the following set of propositions:

1. The state, because of its monopoly on force and on resources, as well as its need to maintain a high level of autonomy, cannot tolerate an autonomous religious domain that might compete with it for loyalty.

2. The state therefore extends its authority to the religious domain and utilizes religious leaders and institutions to perpetuate its policies.

3. The state uses religious values to strengthen its authority and legitimacy.

4. The state will not hesitate to suppress religious institutions if they challenge state authority.

The above propositions are appropriate to the study of the relationship between religion and state in Saudi Arabia. This country is one of the few surviving monarchies whose political and social systems still rest to a great extent on traditional principles and practices. Legitimacy of the ruling House of Saud is primarily based on a combination of tribal and religious factors. More than any other country in the Muslim world, the Saudi kingdom is identified with Islam. Today, the kingdom is considered to be fundamentalist, with the *Quran* as its constitution and the *shari'ah* as the source of its laws and regulations.

With the discovery of oil in the 1930s, change occurred in the areas of education, urbanization, industry, and bureaucracy. The political elite sought to maintain traditional values while seeking material development. This study examines the complex process by which the traditional relationship between religion, society, and polity have been altered in the modern Saudi state and asks two questions for the future: Will there be an increase in differentiation between the roles of religion and state? Or will a modus vivendi and mutual accommodation between the two evolve, in which the state slows down the pace of material change and the religious elite comes to accept some degree of change?

For the purposes of this inquiry, religion is defined as a set of ideas and institutions premised on the belief in the existence of the supernatural. These ideas and institutions influence the ideas and institutions in society and are influenced by them in return. Politics—as state or government—also consists fundamentally of ideas and institutions. The ideology of the political system, the ways in which political decisions are reached, the procedures used to carry out certain tasks, and the expectations about rights and privileges are all important elements to consider. But politics, more than religion, is concerned with societal norms that stipulate how and by whom power shall be used in the pursuit of societal goals. The use of coercive power by government is necessary principally because the available supply of rewards that people strive for, both individually and collectively, is limited. The state, or politics, therefore, may be described as the set of norms and institutions that designates the ultimate coercive power and the process by which power and authority are implemented.

1
Islam: Conflict Between the Vision and Reality

Traditional Islamic political theories are based on the premise that the purpose of government in Islam is to preserve the *shari'ah* and to enforce its dictates. Traditionalists maintain that only God is sovereign and the source of all authority. Consequently, Islam can know no separation between religion and state. Members of the Muslim community (*ummah*) are God's subjects; the community's laws are divine; its property is God's property; its army is God's army; and its enemies are God's enemies.[1] To maintain and enforce the *shari'ah*, a temporal ruler is needed, "whose office is . . . part of the divine plan for mankind."[2] Inasmuch as the Muslim community transcends all cultural and political boundaries and is distinct from and in direct opposition to the community of unbelievers, there must be one ruler to govern the community, and obedience to him is a religious obligation.

The death of Muhammad in 632 A.D., with no succession arranged, confronted the *ummah* with three crises that deeply affected the traditional assumptions in the relationship between religion and state. First, there was the conflict between the Muhajerun and the Ansar, as each group insisted on its right to nominate Muhammad's successor from among its ranks.[3] Second, some tribal leaders argued that their allegiance to Muhammad ended with his death; consequently, they asserted their independence. Third, the civil war between Ali, Muhammad's cousin and son-in-law, and Mu'awiya, governor of Syria, as well as Ali's murder in 661 A.D., permanently shattered the unity of the Islamic community. The schisms that emerged had a direct bearing on the conception of ruler and on the conduct of the state. A number of political theories evolved, all of which were based on the premise that the purpose of government is to maintain the *shari'ah* and enforce its principles, but which differed on who should be caliph and how he should be chosen.[4] These theories focused on the ruler and his relationship to society, used religion and religious symbols to justify the ruler's position, and were written in support or condemnation of one or another ruler. It is the purpose of this chapter to examine the interplay between the Islamic ideal of government and the reality and to relate the results of this interaction to the evolution of government in the modern Arab world.

Historical Setting:
The Islamic Body Politic and the Struggle for Power

The Prophetic State

Muhammad's emigration to Yathrib (Medina) in 622 A.D. marks the beginning of the first Islamic state.[5] This state had a dual character. On the one hand, it was a religious community and as such was defined by its members' acceptance of Muhammad's prophethood and their submission to Islam. On the other hand, it was a political community headed by Muhammad, the statesman. In administering the daily affairs of the *ummah*, Muhammad made a distinction between his religious roles and his temporal ones. All religious matters were to be decided by him alone in accordance with the revelation he received from God. Temporal matters, however, were dealt with in his capacity as the temporal head of the community. This dual character of Muhammad's rule was expressed in his *hadith* (traditional saying): "Whatever concerns your religion bring it forth to me, but for your temporal affairs you may know the best."[6] Putting this principle into practice, Muhammad conducted some of the nonreligious affairs of the community through *shura* (consultation) with his companions. The majority's decision, even if it went against Muhammad's inclination, was implemented. Abu Hurayrah, a close companion of Muhammad and an authority on *hadith*, confirmed this view by stating that in dealing with public matters "nobody could consult his companions as much as the Prophet did."

The Caliphate as an Elective Institution

With his death in 632 A.D., Muhammad's prophetic mission was completed. His legacy consisted of a unified state with a strong drive for expansion. In the leadership of the community, a deputy or successor to Muhammad was needed. Despite the apparent unity of the community, two groups with different social and ideological background emerged—the Muhajerun and the Ansar. Both vied for the leadership of the community, but finally, and after long deliberation, consensus was reached and Abu Bakr, from the Muhajerun, was proclaimed by the elders as Muhammad's successor (*khalifat rasul al-lah*). Except for direct communication with God, the caliph was to maintain the same authority and responsibility as that assumed by Muhammad. He played the religious role of Imam and was the symbol of Islamic unity. As head of the state, the caliph was Prince of the Faithful. It was his responsibility to take charge of all activities related to the internal and external affairs of the state. He was responsible for the maintenance and implementation of the principles of the *shari'ah,* for developing the material welfare of the community, and for defending and expanding the land of Islam. He was accountable for all aspects of state administration and carried out these functions in accordance with the *shari'ah.*[7]

Once Abu Bakr assumed office, he announced the principles that were to guide his government:

> I have been made a ruler over you though I am not the best of you. Help me if I go right, correct me if I go wrong. Truth is faithfulness and falsehood is treachery. The weak one among you will be strong with me till I have got him his due, if God so wills; and the strong one among you will be weak with me till I have made him what he owes, if God so wills. Beware, when a nation gives up its endeavors in the way of God, He makes no exception but brings it low, and when it allows evil to prevail in it, undoubtedly He makes it miserable. Obey me as long as I obey God and His Prophet; if I do not obey them, you owe me no obedience.[8]

Abu Bakr's statement embodies an important principle of Islamic government that was to characterize Islamic political thought even after government had in fact come to be based purely on hereditary succession and perpetuated by methods of force. This principle maintains that obedience to the ruler is binding upon the *ummah* so long as the ruler upholds the *shari'ah;* if he violates or ignores its principles, the community is justified in dismissing him.

Before his death in 634 A.D., Abu Bakr nominated Umar Ibn al-Khattab to succeed him, and his choice was ratified first by the elders of the community and second by the community as a whole. In conducting the affairs of the *ummah,* the Caliph Umar (634–644 A.D.) demonstrated a remarkable ability to apply the principles of the *shari'ah* to new situations created by the expansion of Islam. He encouraged his deputies to base their legal decisions on the *Quran,* the *Sunna* (Muhammad's conduct and *hadith*), and reason. "Do not hesitate," Umar instructed his deputies, "to change a decision once you realize that it was not equitable. This is better than to persevere in error. Be guided by reason."[9] As for deciding a method of succession, Umar appointed an electoral college composed of six prominent community members and delegated to them the duty of choosing the caliph from among themselves.

The Emergence of Factionalism and Development of Hereditary Rule

Following Umar's death, Uthman was elected caliph. Pious and benevolent but weak and undecided, he was dominated by his relatives, and corruption among his officials led to a growing discontent against his rule. In 655 A.D., a delegation from Egypt came to Medina, the capital, and asked Uthman to step down. He refused, claiming for the first time in Muslim history what could be viewed as a divine right to rule. "I shall never take off a mantle," Uthman told his opponents, "that God himself vested me with."[10] Eventually he was murdered; with his death, the religious bond that had held together the Muslim community was irrevocably destroyed.[11]

In the aftermath, Ali was elected to the caliphate, but Mu'awiya and Aisha, Muhammad's wife, refused to pay him allegiance. A long and bloody civil strife ensued, ending with the victory of Mu'awiya and the establishment of the Umayyad dynasty.[12] With the Umayyads in power (661–750 A.D.), the caliphate became a worldly kingship. Its rule, however, ended in 750 A.D., when the Abbasids seized power. Although under Abbasid rule Islamic civilization came into full blossom and the period (750–1258 A.D.) came to be considered "the Golden Age of Islam," the Islamic empire itself fragmented and non-Arab elements dominated the political arena. Whereas all the lands of Islam had once come effectively under the rule of a single caliph, the provinces were now controlled by independent rulers, often hereditarily determined.[13] For example, in 756 A.D., an Umayyad prince, Abd al-Rahman, established his rule over Muslim Spain in defiance of the Abbasid caliph. Following this event in Spain, and between the late eighth and early tenth centuries A.D., other autonomous dynasties emerged in Morocco, Tunisia, eastern Iran, Egypt, Syria, and even parts of Iraq, where the caliphs had established their capital Baghdad. To accommodate the powerful governors of these autonomous regions and maintain the semblance of unity, a tradition developed whereby provincial leaders recognized the titular supremacy of the caliph as head of the Muslim community, who in turn issued them a "diploma of appointment" legitimating their rule.[14] The disintegration of the political system was aggravated by another development. Although historically the land of Islam had been governed by a single caliph, by 929 A.D. there were, for a while, three caliphs: the caliph in Muslim Spain, the Fatimid caliph in Egypt, and the Abbasid caliph in Baghdad.

During Abbasid rule, and because of the influence of non-Arab administrators, some Perso-Byzantine court ceremonies and administrative practices were introduced. Through shrewd and falsified interpretation of some *Quranic* verses, the position of the caliph was glorified. For instance, based on the *Quranic* verse in which God addresses his angels and says, "I am placing in the earth a caliph," meaning Adam, some individuals attempted to place the position of the ruler above that of both the angels and the prophets.[15]

It was during Abbasid rule also that the institution of the ulama evolved. Islam as revealed by Muhammad did not provide for a priesthood, and the caliphs were successors of Muhammad as heads of the community, not as wielders of religious authority. Gradually, however, a body of men developed with specialized religious functions; for the most part, these men were reciters of the *Quran* and experts in the Traditions of Muhammad. A number of theological schools evolved, each with its own interpretation of the principles of the *shari'ah.* With the expansion of Islam during the periods of Umayyad and Abbasid rule, the need for legal scholars and jurists increased.[16] Describing the emergence of the ulama as an institution, William Montgomery Watt wrote:

> If judges were to be taken from men "trained" in the various schools of law, the training had to become . . . formal. Just how this happened is not altogether clear, but some men came to be recognized as authorities in one or other of the specialized religious disciplines which were developing. Those who had been adequately "trained" under recognized masters may be said to have entered the corps of ulama . . . or "scholars" from whom judges and similar officials were selected. This corps of the ulama was the religious institution, and it claimed that it alone (acting through those of its senior members who were recognized as authorities) could formulate the application of the shari'a to particular issues.[17]

Although the ulama claimed to be the sole interpreters of the precepts of the *shari'ah,* they became part of the state administration and consequently lost the autonomy to which they had aspired. In its relationship with the ulama, the state recognized the paramountcy of the *shari'ah,* avoided open contravention of its principles, and occasionally consulted leading ulama and elevated them to positions of authority. On their part, the ulama came to abstain from involvement in political life. When they accepted office, they did so with reluctance. The refusal of the ulama to serve the state was caused primarily by their view of the state as an "oppressor." Al Ghazzali has noted that state revenues have indeed been obtained through oppression and extortion. Anyone, therefore, who accepts a paid position under the state becomes an accomplice in oppression and is thus a sinner.[18] Of course, there are many ulama who have served the political authority, but the general feeling of the ulama body was that the state was a contamination to be avoided.

Decline of the Caliphate Institution and
Emergence of the Sultanate

Theoretically, the caliph and his officials could function only within the confines of the *shari'ah*, as interpreted by the ulama. In practice, however, the ulama were powerless to challenge the abuse of power. In addition, the traditionally powerful and prestigious position of the caliph became restricted by 935 A.D. to heading prayers and sanctioning the authority of de facto rulers in the various provinces of the Abbasid empire. In 946 A.D., for example, the Shi'i-Persian Buwayhids, the new de facto rulers of Baghdad, assumed the title of "amir of amirs" (*amir al-umara*), which came to be a title of imperial sovereignty, distinct from and in practical terms superior to the Abbasid caliph. Independent holders of power also abrogated the title of sultan, so as to demonstrate that they were not appointed by a superior authority.[19] With the Seljuqs in power in the eleventh century, the division of authority between the caliph, as religious head of the community, and the sultan, the ruler responsible for the government, was institutionalized. It was the sultan who would choose and appoint the caliph; then the sultan would swear allegiance to the caliph as head of the community. But it was the sultan who ruled and the caliph who legitimated this rule. In other words, "the Caliph reigned but did not rule; the Sultan did both."[20] The dual authority between the sultan and the caliph ended in 1258 A.D., however, when the Mongol invaders of Iraq executed the Abbasid caliph and abolished the caliphate institution.

From the Mongol invasion on, the sultans ruled alone as the undisputed sovereigns of their state. Meanwhile, the Egyptian Mamluks installed their own "shadow caliphs" long before the title of caliph became one of the many titles used by Muslim rulers. It was not until the nineteenth century, and then only for a brief period, that the Ottoman caliphs laid claim to the allegiance of Muslims. With the continued decline of Ottoman rule, it was only a matter of time before the caliphate institution was abolished. In November 1922, the Grand National Assembly in Ankara deposed Muhammad VI and, two years later, abolished the caliphate.

Ideological Setting: Islamic Thought as a Reaction to Political Factionalism

Movements of Opposition to Islamic Orthodoxy

Differences within the Islamic community, which had begun to emerge during the rule of Uthman, assumed a distinctive theological and political character when Ali took office. The result was civil war. A number of sects and schools of thought evolved, dealing not only with theological issues but also with questions related to the nature of the Islamic state as well as the authority and legality of the caliphate institution. At one extreme, the Shi'is (the Party of Ali) maintained that Muhammad's descendants through the marriage of Fatima to Ali are the sole legitimate inheritors of the caliphate. To these hereditary imams, the Shi'is ascribed not only the divine right of succession but also the exclusive ability to interpret the law properly, since they were by nature infallible. In other words, the Shi'i theory of government posits the necessity of permanent divine guidance of the community through the perpetuation of the prophetic mission by a series of divinely inspired imams, as opposed to the Sunni (Orthodox) view, which claimed the right to install the caliph in the community.

At the other extreme, the puritan Kharijites (Seceders) maintained the right of the community to be the sole judge of the ability of the imam to hold this position. This group asserted that every believer, even a "black slave," could become caliph so long as he is morally and religiously irreproachable in character. They insisted that no tribe or race can enjoy more inherited superiority than another. They particularly opposed the theory of the inherited right of the Quraishites to the caliphate.

The doctrinal beliefs and methods used for the realization of their goals set the Kharijites apart from the majority of Muslims. By resorting to violence, abrogating to themselves the right to be the sole interpreters of the *shari'ah,* and questioning the beliefs of all those who differed with them, the Kharijites turned into a radical minority faction alienated from the Islamic community. Although their slogan was "rule belongs to none but God," they in fact sat in judgment on their fellow Muslims. Their fanaticism ultimately led to their extinction as a political movement.

The extremism and frequent resort to violence of the Shi'is and the Kharijites forced the general body of the Muslim community to adopt positions not only against both armies but against their ideas as well. The excesses of the Kharijites, in particular, contributed to the consecration of the very system against which they revolted and were instrumental in shaping the "authoritarian" theory of government advanced by the Sunni jurists in the tenth and eleventh centuries A.D.

The first reaction to the Kharijites' fanatical idealism was the strengthening of an earlier doctrine put forward by a group of pacifists called the Murji'ites. This group separated religion as belief from religion as works. A believer would remain part of the community, even if he evaded his religious obligations or committed sin. It is not the responsibility of the community, the Murji'ites believed, to determine whether or not a sinner belonged to *Ahl al-Jahim* (the People of Hell) and consequently to expel him from the community. Such a decision is the responsibility of God, to be rendered on the Day of Judgment. In practical terms, this group refused to see in the suppression of the *shari'ah* by the Umayyad caliphs a justifiable cause for denying them the allegiance due to de facto political leaders of Islam. Uthman, Ali, and even Mu'awiya were all servants of God, and by God alone they were to be judged.

The Mu'tazilites and the Ash'arites

Cutting across the Shi'i, Kharijite, and Murji'ite positions are two factions whose religious and political rivalry dominated medieval Islam. The first of these were the Mu'tazilites (Withdrawers), who asserted that he who commits a mortal sin (*kabirah*) secedes from the ranks of the community, but does not become an unbeliever; rather, he occupies a medial position between the two. The second group, the Ash'arites, sought to reconcile the religious ideal of the caliphate with the reality of politics. While the Shi'is asserted the hereditary nature of the Imamate, the Mu'tazilites noted that the community could choose as caliph any morally qualified person, even a non-Quraishi. In opposition to the Murji'ite stand, which rejected the principle of revolt against unjust rulers, the Mu'tazilites regarded it as an obligation on the part of community members to revolt against an unjust caliph, provided that the success of the revolt is certain. Opposed to the Ash'ari view of the caliphate as a religious duty and necessity, the Mu'tazilites noted the rational basis of the caliphate. Some Mu'tazilite writers noted that the enforcement of law is the only raison d'être of the caliphate. If all people observed the *shari'ah*, the scholars remarked, the caliphate would be unnecessary. To the Ash'arites, however, the caliphate commanded obedience simply because it is a divinely inspired institution.

Despite its insistence on reason and free will, the Mu'tazilite movement turned into an instrument of suppression. Under the rule of the Abbasid Caliph al-Ma'mun (813–833 A.D.), the Mu'tazilite creed became the "state religion." In 827 A.D., al-Ma'mun issued a proclamation adopting the Mu'tazilite dogma of the creation of the *Quran*, in opposition to the traditional view that the *Quran* is the identical reproduction of a celestial original. Six years later, the caliph issued an edict stipulating that judges had to pass a test in this dogma. An inquisitorial tribunal for the trial and conviction of those who denied the "creation of the *Quran*" was established, thus initiating the *mihna*. As a result, many ulama removed themselves from state service and began to distinguish clearly between the religious and political spheres. Obviously, Mu'tazilite principles were popular among Abbasid court officials of the period. The movement's end, however, occurred in 848 A.D., when the Abbasid Caliph al-Mutawakil deprived it of court support.

The Attempt to Reconcile Idealism with Reality

The eclipse of the Mu'tazilites was followed by the consolidation of the Ash'ari tradition, which came to be considered the Sunni doctrine of the caliphate. The Sunnis were the latest of all Muslim groups to develop a detailed political theory, which evolved as an apologia for the historical caliphate. Their theory contained, therefore, a blend of abstract general principles deduced from the *shari'ah* as well as provisions derived from the historical experience of Muslims.[21]

The ideological foundation of this theory is the supremacy of the *shari'ah* and the infallible authority of the *ijma'* (consensus of the community). Maintenance and enforcement of the *shari'ah* requires a caliph, whose appointment and obedience are the religious duties of the community. If the caliph violates the dictates of the *shari'ah*, his removal becomes a necessity. Such were the ideal and the principle, but the caliphate became hereditary, rulers deviated from the divine law, and the land of Islam became fragmented. Reacting to the accusations of other factions, and in an obvious attempt to vindicate Sunnism and to preserve the unity of the *ummah*, the ulama rationalized the policies of existing governments. They agreed that "the caliphate was elective, but the caliph could be nominated by his predecessor; the caliph was the sole supreme sovereign of all Islam, but ministers or governors might acquire and hold office by seizure."[22] As the gap between the ideal and reality widened, Sunni ulama continued to rationalize the policies of existing governments until the "tyranny is better than anarchy" principle dominated their writings.[23]

al-Mawardi and al-Ghazzali

A rationalization for the disparity between the theory and practice was provided by al-Mawardi (d. 1058 A.D.), whose *al-Ahkam al-Sultaniya*

(Principles of Government) is treated by Sunni scholars as the classical exposition of Islamic government. This book was written to support the position of the Abbasid caliphs of Baghdad (al-Qadir bi al-Lah, d. 1031, and his successor) against Buwayhid rule. As such, its argument is based on a combination of Islamic tradition and political reality. The caliphate office and its institution, al-Mawardi noted, is a necessary requirement of the *shari'ah* and is not a matter of reason alone. It is an obligatory requirement of the community to appoint an imam. This appointment could be made by one person or by an electoral college whose members should possess specific qualifications.

The caliph himself should also meet certain requirements—majority age, a Quraishi background, physical and mental competency, justice, courage, and knowledge. Once elected, the caliph cannot be displaced in favor of a worthier candidate. In support of the Abbasid position against its opponents, al-Mawardi insisted upon the illegality of having two caliphs rule the land of Islam at the same time. To justify Abbasid hereditary rule, al-Mawardi noted that the assumption of the caliphate in virtue of nomination by the preceding caliph is legal; the nominee, however, must accept the nomination. If the incumbent did not designate a successor, he might limit the choice of the electors after his death to certain persons and designate the electoral college.

Once elected, the caliph should perform specific religious, legal, and military functions. In administering the affairs of the community, the caliph may delegate authority to governors and subordinates, who should act in accordance with the principles of the *shari'ah*. If a governor seizes power—as was the case in most of the governments in al-Mawardi's time—but maintains the *shari'ah* in word and deed, the caliph should grant him recognition. "Necessity dispenses with stipulations which are impossible to fulfill," al-Mawardi wrote.[24]

Maintaining the general principles introduced by al-Mawardi and reflecting the political climate of his time, al-Ghazzali (d. 1111) stated that the jurist is forced to acknowledge the existing power, since the alternative is anarchy and the cessation of social life for lack of a properly constituted authority.

> Which is worse, I ask you [al-Ghazzali wrote] to declare void the Imamates of our days, because of lack of the requisite qualifications, . . . and thus declare that judges are divested of their authority, that all governorships are invalid, that no marriage can be legally contracted and all executive actions in all parts of the [Muslim] world are null and void, and that the people are living in sin; or to say that the Imamate is held by a valid contract, and therefore all executive acts and jurisdictions are valid, given the present circumstances and the necessity of these times?[25]

In his writings, al-Ghazzali acknowledged that de facto authority belongs to the sultan, who with the approval of the ulama designates the caliph. The validity of the sultan's government, however, is dependent upon his oath of allegiance to the caliph and his appointment by the caliph. But satisfactory as this theory might have been to al-Ghazzali and other ulama, the caliphate ceased to have even institutional power, and government by seizure became the pattern until the advance of European rule and the destruction of traditional society occurred. As a result of the continuing disparity between the ideal and reality, Muslim scholars continued to search for answers.

Islamic Reform Movements and the Development of Secularist Tendencies

Islamic movements that sought to reform society have adopted one of two strategies: either (1) to invoke traditional Islamic sources or (2) to reconcile Islamic beliefs with modern notions.[26] One of the earliest movements emerged in eighteenth-century Arabia in the writings and activities of Shaykh Muhammad Ibn Abd al-Wahhab. This was followed by another movement, the Sanusiyah, which appeared in early nineteenth-century North Africa and was manifested in the creation of Sanussi cooperative communities along Islamic lines. The Sanussi movement differed from Wahhabism both in content and approach, although the two are considered to be reformist-fundamentalist in orientation. Both movements, however, provided a point of reference to a more recent generation of reformists who reasserted the overriding authority of the *Quran* and the Traditions.

Unlike the founders of the Wahhabi and Sanussi movements, who were totally inspired by Muslim traditions, other Muslim reformers were influenced by the West and their writings demonstrated this influence. Shaykh Rifa'ah Rafi al-Tahtawi (1801–1873), for example, showed great interest in the European systems of government. He traveled abroad and sought to popularize European ideas and techniques in Egypt.[27]

In addition to writing a number of books himself, al-Tahtawi translated, with the help of his students, some two hundred books and pamphlets. These were published by the first Arabic printing press, established in 1822 in the outskirts of Cairo.[28] In his writings, al-Tahtawi demonstrated his belief that the ruler should possess extensive power but act in accordance with the dictates of the *shari'ah* and the public interest. He maintained that the subjects, on the other hand, owed allegiance to the ruler as a corollary to their obedience to God and the Prophet.[29] As for the role of the ulama in the Islamic state, al-Tahtawi urged them to be innovative, to adapt the *shari'ah* to new circumstances. He also noted the similarity between the principles of the *shari'ah* and those of natural law on which the legal codes of modern Europe are based. This identification enabled him to legitimize recourse to other systems of law so as to modernize Islamic law.

Al-Tahtawi's attempt to modernize Islamic law and society was further pursued by Jamal al-Din al-Afghani and Muhammad Abduh, who appeared in the latter part of the nineteenth century. Muhammad Ali (1805–1849), the founder of modern Egypt, did not attempt to reform the old centers of religious learning. Instead, he created a parallel system of schools along Western lines. Since army officers, civil servants, and government officials were recruited from these new schools, the religious institutions continued to decline and to attract only the mediocre students. The result was the creation of two distinct educated classes in Egypt: (1) the traditional ulama, deriving their knowledge from old manuals, commentaries, and texts, and (2) the modern Western-educated class. Both were incapable of reinterpreting Islam in the light of modern conditions. It was at this critical moment that Shaykh Muhammad Abduh appeared. Abduh asserted that the *Quran* yielded categorical guidance in matters of worship, but also that it prescribed only general principles in the area of human relations. As a reformer, Abduh was a gradualist. He maintained that the Islamic response to Western pressures, whether cultural or political, was education—not revolt.

On the political front, Abduh wrote that the *Quranic* command to obey lawful authority was misunderstood by the people to mean unconditional obedience to the leaders. They failed to realize that their duty to obey was predicated on the ruler himself being committed to follow the rule of law and to wield power in the interest of the people.[30] Islam, Abduh noted, does not ascribe infallibility to the ruler, who is not a theocrat and does not possess a divine right to rule.

The works of Muhammad Abduh proved to his contemporaries the legitimacy and, indeed, the duty to interpret the *shari'ah* in all aspects relating to worldly affairs. One of the immediate results of Abduh's writings and activities was the emergence of a reformist movement, which, under the leadership of Abduh's disciple and biographer Rashid Rida, was to gravitate gradually toward the rigidity of Wahhabism. Like other reformers, Rida and his movement called for the reactivation of *ijtihad* as a point of departure toward the adaptation of the *shari'ah* to modern conditions as well as toward the restoration of the caliphate. However, the movement's rigid fundamentalism prevented it from realizing its objectives.

In contrast to Rida's conservative views and his call to restore the caliphate, the Western-educated Azharite Ali Abd al-Raziq published *al-Islam wa Usul al-Hukum* in 1925. In this text he noted that there is no specific form of government that can be called Islamic; he also rejected the need for the caliphate.[31] So unorthodox were the views of Abd al-Raziq that the Grand Council of al-Azhar tried him and ultimately expelled him from this foremost seat of Islamic learning. Abd al-Raziq rejected the traditional view that the caliphate was necessary and that Muslims were under an obligation to nominate or choose a caliph. The institution of the caliphate, he noted, has no canonical basis, in either the *Quran* or the *shari'ah*. The author further noted that the verses often cited to give the caliphate a religious sanctity mean no more than that among Muslims there must be some leaders to whom the affairs of the community should be entrusted. Moreover, no consensus on the need to establish or maintain the caliphate was reached. Abd al-Raziq indicated that there were dissenting voices even at the time the first caliph was selected and that consensus was never established by the jurists. The views of the Kharijites and some Mu'tazilites—that the duty of Muslims is to obey the *shari'ah*, and also that if all the members of the *ummah* could maintain justice among themselves there would be no need even for government—support this view. Historical evidence shows that the caliphate was always seized by force rather than brought about through election, as Abd al-Raziq noted. Even when a consensus on its establishment was formally obtained, it was invalid as canonical proof since it was always elicited under duress. Abd al-Raziq emphasized the view that Islam was a universal religion and that it did not need the protection of universal power.

The most important implication of Abd al-Raziq's study is the separation between religion and state. From an orthodox point of view his position was revolutionary, for he insisted that Islam was a purely spiritual religion, that the political office of Muhammad was not an essential part of his prophetic office, and that the caliphate, as a temporal and spiritual institution, was not necessary.

A quarter of a century following Abd al-Raziq's condemnation, the call for the separation between religion and state was raised again by Khalid M. Khalid in his book *Min Huna Nabda'*.[32] Khalid, however, remained attached, like Abd al-Raziq, to the traditional faith of Islam, the spiritual basis of which he appears anxious to preserve. The difference between the two advocates of the separation between religion and state is that Khalid, while endorsing the secular thesis of Abd al-Raziq, is not content with subtle theological polemics but attacks the ulama themselves and advocates their total expulsion from public life. In the words of Khalid, "there is no other course open to governments and societies which respect themselves than to rapidly exclude this insidious priesthood from their midst, by all means at their disposal, and to cleanse religion from all the corrupt elements clinched to it."[33] By doing so, Khalid continued, adherence to religion will be safeguarded. To eliminate the religious establishment is no easy task. The ulama have succeeded through deceptive means in entrenching themselves in society. One of their subtle methods is to preach "holy poverty" and resignation in the name of religion. Khalid further noted that they also condone social injustice and popular misery and suffering as the inevitable dictates of Providence, which must be borne with fortitude in preparation for the eternal happiness of the world to come.

In his study of Muslim history, Khalid concluded that the theocratic state has been an instrument of repression and intimidation throughout the ages. He also claimed that it has failed in maintaining Islamic principles, and that those who aspire to revive it are the misguided fanatics who desire to surrender the freedoms of thought and belief that have been won at the cost of many sacrifices. Finally, Khalid maintained that the curtailment of ecclesiastical authority and the separation of religion and state are two necessary conditions for all forms of progress and an ultimate safeguard to the survival of religion itself. Religion is a body of spiritual truths that are universally and permanently valid and are accordingly independent of the conditions of change or development. Political systems and political objectives, on the other hand, are not static; moreover, although they might apply to one period, they may not be valid for another.[34]

Conclusion

Insofar as traditional Islamic political theory maintains that religion and state are one and indivisible, no proper study of Muslim politics can be either complete or realistic unless it is examined in relation to religion. With this fact in mind, the first chapter has examined the historical and theoretical development of the relationship between religion and state in Islam. The main objective was to search for answers to these ever-present questions: What is an Islamic state? What kind of relationship exists between the religious and political spheres in that state? According to Islamic traditional political theory, the purpose of the state is to maintain the *shari'ah* and enforce its ordinances. The political authority is obliged not only to accept the *shari'ah*, but also to maintain and enforce its principles. Such was the theory, but the reality of Muslim politics was different. By the end of the first Islamic century, tension between vision and reality heightened, and government by seizure became the order of the day.

There are several underlying causes for the continued disparity between the religious ideal and reality. First, although the *shari'ah* was originally a progressive instrument to further Islam, it gradually lost its dynamism and degenerated into a rigid, archaic law as a consequence of the ulama's inability to innovate and adapt religious law to reality. Second, while there was an institutional de facto separation between religion and state, Islamic political thought continued to claim the existence of a fusion of religious and political functions performed by a unitary structure. As for the ulama themselves, they never gave up their claim to influence political authority. The secular rulers tacitly accepted this claim in order to receive the ulama's consent and approval of their authority.

The ulama's failure to adapt the *shari'ah* to changing circumstances is revealed in the organizational structure of their establishment. As Donald Eugene Smith has noted, a relatively low level of ecclesiastical organization has existed among Muslim ulama. This low level of organization renders the ulama's response to change less coherent and effective than if they were highly structured.[35] Third, the preservation of the socioreligious order is delegated to the political authority, which is dominant in society. As a result, the ulama have, with some exceptions, depended on the state for their survival. Indeed, the ulama's *raison d'être* was tied to the state's function of enforcing the *shari'ah*. Resulting from this symbiotic relationship between the ulama and the state, the ulama's political participation was confined to the accepted and legitimate level of political activity.

The disintegration of the Ottoman empire and the advance of European imperialism into the Muslim world, as well as the resultant disruption of the traditional system, altered the historical pattern of the relationship between religion and state. Whereas in the past governments needed religion to legitimate their rule, they became less dependent on religion in the nation-state period as new sources of legitimacy emerged. This, however, was not the only change. Stephen Humphreys noted that three main responses to the breakdown of the traditional society have manifested themselves in the Arab world: (1) the fundamentalist response, (2) the religious-modernist response, and (3) the secularist response.[36]

The fundamentalist response to this disruption of modern society maintains that "change must be governed by traditional values and modes of understanding." The Wahhabi and Sanussi movements are an example of this trend. The proponents of the second response, which was manifested by the emergence of the religious-modernist trend, engaged in a search for accommodation of the *shari'ah* with the needs of modern life. Al-Tahtawi, for example, pointed out the progressive character of the *shari'ah* and insisted that many of its aspects are suitable for contemporary life. Finally, the secularist response, as projected in the writings of Khalid, held that the political obligations of the individual should not be defined by his religious affiliation.

The unity of the religious and political spheres advocated by Islam has existed primarily at the theoretical level rather than in practice. There has always been a startling disparity between the ideal and the reality of Islamic government. The Wahhabi movement arose to protest this disparity and to initiate a new political experiment. It succeeded in forming the state of Saudi Arabia and continues even today to provide it with ideological legitimacy. In sum, this study of the relationship between religion and state in the Kingdom of Saudi Arabia has examined the manner in which the Islamic ideal affected the politics of the kingdom and the extent to which this ideal has been realized.

Wahhabism and the Formation
of the Saudi State:
Realization of the Vision

The founding of new religious formations invariably ushers in a measure of social discord. The development of this discord depends on the extent to which these formations challenge the established norms and institutions. The challenge is most apparent when an attempt is made to redefine the boundaries and membership of a new community and to establish a new code of behavior for followers or advocate a revival of old beliefs. Understandably, such attempts lead their proponents to break with the past; they entail the development of belief systems, rituals, and organizational structures that differentiate these groups from other religious groups.

To ensure their survival and expansion, new religious movements cannot remain oblivious to the political sphere. A relationship of either mutual dependency or confrontation evolves between these movements and the existing political authority, depending on whether common or exclusive objectives develop. Religious movements might seek, for instance, the protection and help that the institutions of state can offer and, in return, provide these same institutions with legitimation and support. Even when a policy of interdependence is pursued, the relationship that emanates is often subject to serious strains. "This fact of mutual dependence of relatively autonomous spheres," noted S. N. Eisenstadt in his wide-ranging survey of the political relationships of religion in centralized empires, "could easily create many tensions between them as each would desire to control those structural positions of the other through which it could provide its own needs."[1] In other words, the religious and political institutions are potential competitors both for economic and manpower resources and for the active political engagement and support of different groups and strata in society.

This chapter examines the rise, ideology, and consolidation of Wahhabism and the relationship between its founder, Shaykh Muhammad Ibn Abd al-Wahhab, and his political patron, Amir Muhammad Ibn Saud and his successor, Amir Abd al-Aziz Ibn Saud. The bond between shaykh and prince was forged in 1745. It provided Ibn Abd al-Wahhab with a political arm for his religious teachings and assured Al Saud of sanction from a recognized theologian as well as a body of converts, which could be used to expand political authority and control of the Arabian Peninsula. More specifically, the following questions will be addressed in this chapter: (1) What is Wahhabism? (2) How did the established religiopolitical orders react to its emergence and principles? (3) What role did it play in the formation and consolidation of the Saudi state? (4) What was the nature and outcome of the relationship between the shaykh and the prince?

Muhammad Ibn Abd al-Wahhab

Eighteenth-century Arabia existed within the domain of the Ottoman empire. Ottoman officials, however, did not exercise effective control beyond the regions bordering the Red Sea and the pilgrimage route. Najd and the area eastward led a sovereign form of existence in which the various districts were ruled by local chiefs. The region was characterized by political fragmentation and incessant tribal conflicts. Religious beliefs and practices had deviated from Orthodox Islam. The Najdi historian Ibn Bishr wrote in the eighteenth century that

> it was common for trees and rocks to be invested with supernatural powers; tombs were venerated and shrines were built near them; and all were regarded as sources of blessing and objects of vows. . . . Moreover, swearing by other than God, and similar forms of both major and minor polytheism were widely practiced.[2]

It was into this environment that Muhammad Ibn Abd al-Wahhab was born in 1703, in al-Uyayna in Najd. He belonged to a prestigious family of jurists, both theologians and *qadis* (judges). Under the tutorship of his father, young Muhammad studied Hanbali jurisprudence and read classical works on *tafsir* (exegesis), *hadith* (tradition), and *tawhid* (monotheism). In his early twenties, Muhammad began to denounce what he described as the polytheistic beliefs and practices of his society. He rejected "the corruption and laxity of the contemporary decline . . . [and] insisted solely on the [*shari'ah*]."[3]

The beliefs of Muhammad Ibn Abd al-Wahhab alienated him from the establishment ulama and led to the dismissal of his father from the *qada* (judgeship). Subsequently, Ibn Abd al-Wahhab's family, including his father, had to leave al-Uyayna for neighboring Huraymila in 1726. Muhammad remained in al-Uyayna for a while, but because the ulama "were able to defame his call and reputation, and instigate the common folk who beset him with ridicule, abuse, and insults," he left al-Uyayna for Hejaz.[4]

In Hejaz, Muhammad made his pilgrimage to Mecca and Medina, where he attended lectures on different branches of Islamic learning. Ibn Bishr reported that he studied under Shaykh Abd Allah Ibn Ibrahim Ibn Sayf and Shaykh Hayat al-Sindi, both of whom were admirers of the Hanbali Ibn Taymiya. Like Ibn Taymiya, Sayf and Sindi opposed *taqlid* (imitation), which was commonly accepted by the followers of the four Sunni schools of jurisprudence. Both scholars felt the urgent need to reform the socioreligious situation of Muslims in Najd and elsewhere.[5] Their teachings had a great impact on Muhammad, who began to take a more aggressive attitude toward the establishment ulama.

Another important event that seemed to have influenced the intellectual evolution of Muhammad Ibn Abd al-Wahhab was his visit to Basra. There he widened his study of *hadith* and jurisprudence and came into contact with the Shi'ites, who venerated Ali's shrine in al-Najaf and the tomb of Hussein in neighboring Karbala. Ibn Abd al-Wahhab's call to reform the Muslim world was rejected by the ulama of both Basra and Karbala, and he was ultimately forced to leave the area.[6]

Muhammad Ibn Abd al-Wahhab returned to Huraymila to rejoin his father and immediately began to criticize the innovations and polytheistic acts practiced by the Najdis and others. His criticism seems to have been so bitter that he was met with strong opposition from the ulama and even his own father. During this period, Muhammad composed his most famous work, *Kitab al-Tawhid* (Book of Monotheism), copies of which circulated quickly and widely in Najd.[7]

The Shaykh and the Prince:
An Alliance That Failed

The year 1740 witnessed the death of Muhammad Ibn Abd al-Wahhab's father and the consolidation of the Wahhabi movement.[8] The death of his father allowed the shaykh to adopt a more aggressive line, because he felt less constrained than before.[9] He declared war on those who by word or act were violating the doctrine of monotheism. In a relatively short time, the influence of Muhammad Ibn Abd al-Wahhab spread widely. The consolidation of his movement took place when the ruler of al-Uyayna, Uthman Ibn Mu'ammar, offered him protection. The shaykh accepted the invitation to reside in al-Uyayna both because it allowed him to return to the place of his birth where his family enjoyed a high social status and because it provided the protection he needed to propagate his ideology. To cement his ties with the town's leader, the shaykh married al-Jawhara, Uthman's aunt.

The ruler of al-Uyayna ordered his townsmen to observe the teachings of Muhammad Ibn Abd al-Wahhab. Once the protection of a political leader was secured, the shaykh implemented the principles of his call. Among his earliest acts was the destruction of the spot where Zayd Ibn al-Khatab was believed to be buried, as well as the tombs of other Companions of the Prophet Muhammad, all of whom were objects of veneration. He also revived the Islamic law of stoning an adulterous woman to death.[10] Both incidents mark the establishment of a Wahhabi society in which the doctrines of *tawhid* were strictly observed.

The shaykh's activities, and the protection he received from the leader of al-Uyayna, antagonized the ulama of the region and led them to intensify their attacks on the Wahhabi movement. Ibn Ghanam, a Najdi historian and contemporary of Muhammad Ibn Abd al-Wahhab, quoted the charges made by Ibn Suhaym, the judge of Riyadh and a leading opponent of Wahhabism, against the shaykh:

> He burned the book *Dala'il al-Khayrat*[11] because its author referred to the Prophet as our master and our lord . . . ; he also burned the work *Rawd al-Rayahin* and renamed it Rawd al-Shayatin.[12] He says that the people have not been following the religion . . . ; he does not consider the differences of view among the religious imams as mercy but as misfortune . . . ; he abandoned the praise of the Sultan in the Friday sermon, claiming that he is dissolute . . . ; he considers as innovation the *salat* [prayers] for the Prophet on Friday.[13]

The shaykh accused the ulama of opposing his movement because they feared the loss of social prestige and reputation. He reproached them for not taking the initiative in criticizing offensive practices that he considered un-Islamic. He also attributed the opposition of the ulama to his denunciation of the acceptance by the *qadis* of payment from persons who sought their legal advice or arbitration.[14] The ulama of the region intensified their attacks on the shaykh and warned the rulers that "it was their obligation, as Muslim leaders responsible for the preservation of the shari'ah, to put an end to Wahhabi errors and innovations." Pointing to the threatening character of the movement, the ulama noted that the shaykh's purpose was "nothing less than to stir up the common folks to revolt against the authority of the established leaders."[15]

The appeal to eliminate the Wahhabi movement found a positive response from Sulayman Ibn Muhammad, tribal leader of the Banu Khalid and ruler of the al-Ahsa region. Sulayman was concerned with the rapidly increasing number of followers who joined the Wahhabis. Ibn Bishr noted that Sulayman wrote to Uthman Ibn Mu'ammar, ruler of al-Uyayna, demanding that the shaykh be expelled or killed. If not, Sulayman warned, all economic assistance to al-Uyayna would be cut off.[16] Fearful of Sulayman's reprisal, the ruler of al-Uyayna terminated his alliance with the shaykh and expelled him from the town.

The Shaykh and the Prince:
An Alliance That Succeeded

After his expulsion from al-Uyayna, Ibn Abd al-Wahhab sought refuge in Dar'iya. Its rulers were in conflict with Sulayman Ibn Muhammad, and, more important, the shaykh's doctrine had already been adopted by some notables of the town, among whom were the brothers and sons of Muhammad Ibn Saud, the ruler.

Shortly after his arrival in Dar'iya, the shaykh was visited by Muhammad Ibn Saud, who offered him "protection equal to that of the chief's own women and children."[17] In return for his support, the ruler of Dar'iya asked the shaykh not to leave Dar'iya once other towns began following his teachings and not to oppose his taxation of the inhabitants of the principality. Ibn Abd al-Wahhab agreed to the first condition but, reluctant to give a clear answer to the second, he said: ". . . may God grant you victories, the booty from which will be greater than these taxes."[18] The agreement arrived at between the shaykh and the prince may be considered the cornerstone of the Wahhabi-Saudi alliance, according to which, as indicated by the author of *Lam' al-Shihab*, the temporal power was left to Muhammad Ibn Saud and his successors whereas the spiritual was reserved for Muhammad Ibn Abd al-Wahhab and his descendants.

The shaykh spent the first two years at Dar'iya propagating his views and writing letters to various rulers, scholars, and tribal leaders of the peninsula.[19] The response he elicited was as much a product of political and economic considerations as it was a matter of religious dogma. Some leaders joined the new movement because they saw it as a means of gaining an ally against their local rivals. Others feared that their acceptance of the call would diminish their authority in favor of Ibn Saud and oblige them to pay him at least part of the revenues that they collected from their subjects.

By 1746, the time seemed ripe for Al Saud and the shaykh to resort to force in order to achieve what they had not been able to do by means of persuasion and argument. The shaykh's prestige was now firmly established. The inhabitants of the region had been indoctrinated to believe that opponents of the Wahhabi cause were enemies of Islam who should be fought and whose properties were lawful spoil.

Since the region was beyond the reach of organized political authority, it offered the Wahhabis the opportunity to pursue their designs by military means. Muhammad Ibn Abd al-Wahhab and Muhammad Ibn Saud declared *jihad* (holy war) on their opponents. One principality after another fell under the attacks of the Saudi forces. By 1773 the principality of Riyadh had fallen, and its properties were incorporated by the treasury of Dar'iya.

The fall of Riyadh marked a new period in the career of Muhammad Ibn Abd al-Wahhab. He delegated some of his power to Abd al-Aziz Ibn Muhammad Ibn Saud, who succeeded his father in 1765, and concentrated on teaching and worship until his death in 1791. The death of Muhammad Ibn Abd al-Wahhab did not stop the expansion of the new state, however. The movement not only resisted its opponents and gained territories in neighboring principalities, but it was also able, within a relatively short period, to subjugate both Mecca and Medina, which were captured in 1805 and 1806, respectively.

Wahhabi Doctrine

The shaykh wrote on a variety of Islamic subjects such as theology, exegesis, jurisprudence, and the life of the Prophet. His works consisted of books, treatises, letters, and sermons. A set of issues dominated the teachings of Muhammad Ibn Abd al-Wahhab and distinguished Wahhabism from other Islamic movements—namely, (1) *tawhid* (monotheism), (2) *tawasul* (intercession), (3) *ziyarat al-qubur* (visitation of graves and erection of tombs), (4) *takfir* (charge of unbelief), (5) *bid'a* (innovation), and (6) *ijtihad* and *taqlid* (original juristic opinions and imitation). Although this chapter is not concerned with the study of theological differences and disagreements between the Wahhabis and their opponents, it is necessary to outline the main ideological characteristics of the movement as they have influenced the development of the Saudi state and shaped its Islamic character.

Tawhid

Tawhid is the central theme in the Wahhabi doctrine. Muhammad Ibn Abd al-Wahhab considered it "the eternal religion of God"; indeed, it is "the religion of Islam itself."[20] The shaykh maintained that the unity of God reveals itself in three distinct ways. First, there is *tawhid al-rububiyah*, which is the assertion of the unity of God and His action. "He alone is the Creator, the Provider and Disposer of the universe."[21] The second is *tawhid al-asma' wa al-sifat*. This concept deals with God's characteristics. He is "The Beneficent, the Merciful . . . , the One"; He is "the Knowledgeable."[22] He is "established on the Throne,"[23] and "unto Him belongeth whatsoever is in the heavens and whatsoever is in the earth, and whatsoever is between them, and whatsoever is beneath the sod."[24]

The third aspect in *tawhid* is described as *tawhid al-Ilahiya*. Worship of God should be to God alone: "There is no god but Allah, and man should . . . serve thy lord till the inevitable cometh unto thee."[25] The assertion that "there is no god but Allah and Muhammad is the Prophet of God" means that all forms of worship should be devoted solely to God; Muhammad is not to be worshipped but, as an apostle, should be obeyed and followed.[26] The shaykh maintained that Muslims should distinguish between God, the Lord and Creator, and the Prophet, the servant and created. By virtue of his Prophethood, however, Muhammad occupies an exceptional position among all humans. He is infallible, and Muslims should follow his way in faith and behavior.[27]

Tawasul

Wahhabis strongly disagreed with their opponents on the question of intercession. For Muhammad Ibn Abd al-Wahhab, *ibada* (worship) refers to "all the utterances and actions—inward as well as outward— that God desires and commands."[28] In *Kitab al-Tawhid*, the shaykh wrote that to seek protection from trees, stones, and the like is a major polytheistic practice. Similarly, help or aid and protection or refuge are not to be sought from anyone except God. Intercession, the shaykh further noted, cannot be granted without God's permission and His satisfaction with the one for whom it is asked, who has to be a true monotheist. The intercession commonly sought from dead saints is prohibited. As for invoking the Prophet to intercede for individuals before God, Muhammad Ibn Abd al-Wahhab pointed out that the Prophet Muhammad was neither able to guide those he liked to Islam without the will of God nor allowed to ask forgiveness from Him for polytheists.[29] The shaykh warned believers against showing excessive devotion to saints and the use of their graves as places of worship.[30]

Ziyarat al-Qubur

The doctrine of intercession led the Wahhabis to view with utter indignation the widely followed practices of grave visitation and the building of domes near graves. To start with, Shaykh Muhammad Ibn Abd al-Wahhab considered visitation, if performed in the true spirit of Islam, to be a pious and praiseworthy act.[31] Practices of visitation are deemed by the Wahhabis to be either recommended or objectionable. The former are considered to be in accordance with the teachings of the Prophet and are said to serve three purposes: (1) as a reminder of the world-to-come; (2) as a source of mutual benefit for both the visitor—because of his observance of the Prophet's tradition—and the visited, because of the prayers offered; and (3) as a means of keeping alive the memory of the dead.

People, the shaykh wrote, have changed the prayers for the dead to prayers *to* the dead; grave sites have become places of assembly for worship. The excessive veneration of the deceased who enjoyed a holy reputation, the shaykh noted further, was the first step toward idol-worship in the pre-Islamic period.[32] To avoid polytheism, the Wahhabis considered it an obligation to destroy all the tombs that had already been built. They insisted that burial grounds should be level with the ground and that writings, decoration, or illumination of graves should be avoided.[33]

Takfir and Qital

The Wahhabi doctrine of *takfir* states that mere affiliation with Islam is not sufficient in itself to prevent a Muslim from becoming a polytheist. Moreover, the person who utters the *shahada* (proclamation of faith) and still practices polytheism, as defined by the Wahhabis, should be denounced as an infidel and killed.[34] In support of this position, the shaykh listed certain *Quranic* verses indicating that the "hypocrites" uttered the *shahada*, performed the daily prayers, and even fought alongside the Prophet. Yet, they "will be in the lowest depth of the fire, and thou wilt find no helper for them."[35] In a letter written by Muhammad Ibn Abd al-Wahhab to one of his opponents, Sulayman Ibn Suhaym, he defined an infidel as the one "who has known the religion of the Prophet and yet stands against it, prevents others from accepting it and shows hostility to those who follow it."[36] As for fighting, the shaykh considered it the duty of every able believer to fight infidels and "hypocrite" Muslims.

Bid'a

Innovation is defined by the Wahhabis as any doctrine or action not based on the *Quran,* the Traditions, or the authority of the Companions.[37] The shaykh condemned all forms of innovation and rejected the views of those who maintained that an innovation could be good or praiseworthy. He invoked the authority of the *Quran* and the Traditions of Muhammad to support his views. In *Usul al-Islam,* Muhammad Ibn Abd al-Wahhab quoted the *Quranic* verse: "Verily, in the messenger of Allah ye have a good example for him who looketh unto Allah and the Last Day, and remembereth Allah much."[38] This verse, according to Muhammad Ibn Abd al-Wahhab, enjoins Muslims to base all their beliefs and acts on the *Quran,* the word of God. The shaykh also quoted the Prophet as saying: "Every *muhditha* (innovation) is bid'a, and ever bid'a leads astray."[39] The Wahhabis rejected as *bid'a* such acts as celebrating the Prophet's birth, seeking intercession from saints, reciting the *fatiha* ("the opening"—i.e., of the *Quran*) on behalf of the founders of Sufi orders after the five daily prayers, and performing the five daily prayers all over again after the final Friday prayer in the month of Ramadan.

Ijtihad and Taqlid

According to Shaykh Muhammad Ibn Abd al-Wahhab and his followers, God commanded people to obey Him alone and to follow the teachings of the Prophet. This complete adherence to the *Quran* and the Traditions, which the Wahhabis demanded of Muslims, entailed also a rejection of all interpretations offered by the four schools of Islamic jurisprudence (*madhahib*)—including the Wahhabis' own Hanbali school if it was not in accordance with the two prime sources.[40]

The Wahhabis developed strict procedures to direct the discussion of doctrinal issues. In judging religious questions, they will first search the texts of the *Quran* and the Traditions and define their views accordingly. If reference is not found in these texts, they will look for the consensus of the "Virtuous Ancestors," particularly the "Companions and Their Successors," and the *ijma'* (consensus) of the scholars. *Ijma',* however, is restricted only to those who follow the *Quran* and the Traditions.

As for *ijtihad,* the Wahhabis reject the idea that the "doors of *ijtihad*" are closed. Although they follow the Hanbali school, they do not accept its precepts as final. If any Hanbali interpretation can be proven wrong, then it must be abandoned. In support of their argument, the Wahhabis quote *Quranic* verses, which stress that the *Quran* and the Traditions constitute the only bases of Islamic law.

Wahhabism and the Dynamics of Power

When Shaykh Muhammad Ibn Abd al-Wahhab launched his movement in the 1720s, he denounced the social values and religious
practices of his society. He accused Najdi political leaders of not
enforcing the dictates of the *shari'ah.* The movement gathered converts
because it "advocated something old in a new way."[41] Indeed, as A.
D. Nock has indicated, "the originality of a prophet lies commonly
in his ability to fuse into a white heat combustible material which is
there, to express and to appear to meet the half formed prayers of
at least some of his followers."[42] Wahhabism advocated the old Islam
in a new cloak—both militant and uncompromising. The success of
the movement, and its transformation into a state ideology, took place
when Muhammad Ibn Abd al-Wahhab allied himself with the rulers
of Dar'iya. The alliance provided Wahhabism with needed support
and protection and offered Ibn Saud the ideological platform and
recruits needed to effect his designs. Attacks on neighboring principalities, and, indeed, on the whole of the peninsula, were justified
by the invocation of the tradition of *takfir* and *qital.* More important,
Wahhabi teachings justified and consolidated Saudi rule over Arabia.
In his writings, Muhammad Ibn Abd al-Wahhab stressed that obedience
to rulers is obligatory, even if such rulers are oppressive. The rulers'
commands should be followed as long as they do not contradict the
rules of religion, of which the ulama are the interpreters. The shaykh
advised patience with the oppression of rulers and denounced armed
rebellion against them.[43] He also warned the rulers to be just, however.
The ruler's main objective, the shaykh wrote, should be the application
of the *shari'ah,* and this can be accomplished through cooperation
with the ulama.

The views of Muhammad Ibn Abd al-Wahhab on the role of the
ulama in the Islamic state are based on Ibn Taymiya's definition of
the ideal Islamic state as containing two holders of authority: the
ulama and the umara. Because of their knowledge of Islamic law the
ulama constitute the premier directive class in the community, and
the rulers must govern with their advice and cooperation. Neither
Ibn Taymiya nor Muhammad Ibn Abd al-Wahhab, however, suggested
that the ulama should constitute a sacred clergy or enjoy special
privileges. In brief, the ruler is responsible for the upholding of correct
religious obligations, which are expected of Muslim rulers—the fast,
the prayers, the pilgrimage, the application of *hudud* (punishments),
the collection of *zakat* (alms-giving), and so on. The ulama, on the
other hand, are to advise the ruler and support him as long as he
applies the word of God. As Ibn Taymiya suggested, "the authority

to rule over people is obtained either by their willing obedience to the imam or by his compulsion over them. And when he becomes able to rule over them . . . , he becomes the ruler, to whom obedience is due, as long as he orders obedience to Allah."[44]

The relationship between Muhammad Ibn Abd al-Wahhab and the rulers of Dar'iya corresponded closely to the principle of cooperation advocated by Ibn Taymiya. The Najdi historian Ibn Bishr noted that the shaykh's authority was as important as that of the amir.

> A fifth of all the booty, the alms and all revenues brought to Dar'iya was handed over to Muhammad Ibn Abd al-Wahhab, who would use them at his discretion. Neither Abd al-Aziz nor anyone else received anything without his permission. The moves for peace as well as the moves for war were made by him. The opinions and statements made by Muhammad Ibn Saud and his son, Abd al-Aziz, were based on the Shaykh's statements and thinking.[45]

Although Najdi sources inform us that Muhammad Ibn Abd al-Wahhab delegated some of his power to Abd al-Aziz in 1774, they fail to indicate the reasons for this decision. What is known, however, is that Abd al-Aziz continued to consult the shaykh on major matters. Moreover, religious and educational affairs remained under the direct supervision of Muhammad Ibn Abd al-Wahhab. Linked to religious affairs, and falling under the shaykh's jurisdiction as well, was the justice system. The shaykh appointed the *mutawi'a* (religious-morality enforcers), who served as the enforcers of justice and were financed by the public treasury. Any community member who did not fulfill his religious obligations or who violated the principles of the *shari'ah* was harshly punished.

According to Muhammad Ibn Abd al-Wahhab, as well as Ibn Taymiya and other Muslim scholars, Islam is based on the principle of "Commanding the Good and Forbidding Evil." The observance of this principle is an obligatory duty for Muslim leaders and every Muslim capable of its exercise. To enforce this principle, the Wahhabis instituted the *mutawi'a* network. Each *mutawi'* was assigned to a district, and his duties included the enforcement of public attendance of prayers and prevention of objectionable acts (e.g., drinking alcohol, smoking tobacco, wearing silk clothes or gold jewelry, and playing or listening to music). This system proved successful in controlling the society and consolidating Saudi rule. Each *mutawi'* was instructed to compose a list of names of all adult male members of his district. At each prayer, names were called out in the mosque. Absent members were visited at their homes by the *mutawi'*, the imam, and some leading members of the community. Repeated abstention from public prayers invited reprimand or penalty.

Conclusion

When Muhammad Ibn Abd al-Wahhab began his movement in the 1720s, his immediate objectives were to gain recognition and protection from a political leader in the Arabian Peninsula. The alliance he forged with Prince Muhammad Al Saud in 1740 fulfilled both objectives. It provided Al Saud with an ideological rationalization of their rule in Arabia.

Once the Saudi state became institutionalized, the shaykh continued to play an important role in the affairs of the polity. Indeed, Al Saud found the doctrinal formulations of Ibn Abd al-Wahhab to be highly instrumental in the propagation of their rule. The dependency on religious movements for legitimacy of Muslim political leaders, including the Saudis of the eighteenth century, is not surprising. The Abbasid and Fatimid caliphs, for example, came to power on the crest of religious movements. What is surprising, however, is that the relationship between religion and state in eighteenth-century Arabia was harmonious. Both the religious and political spheres shared a complementarity of objectives. The existence of one was dependent on the survival and continued support of the other. The durability of this alliance, however, needs to be tested by reference to twentieth-century developments, when Ibn Saud resurrected the Saudi kingdom. The question is this: To what extent can the modern state, given its monopoly of force and resources and its need to maintain a high level of autonomy, tolerate an autonomous religious domain that could compete with it for loyalty?

Part 2

Religion and State in Patrimonial Society

Introduction

All forms of political domination are admixtures of charismatic, traditional, or legal authority. The specification and attributes of these ideal type categories provide a useful analytic tool for the comparison, classification, and understanding of political systems.[1] Charismatic authority may be defined as a certain quality of an individual personality by virtue of which its holder is "set apart from ordinary men and treated as endowed with supernatural, superhuman, or at least specifically exceptional powers or qualities."[2] To be a charismatic leader, the individual must be viewed by his followers as such, and from time to time he must demonstrate his leadership qualities. If he fails to do so over a long period, his charismatic authority may erode or disappear altogether.

Traditional domination is based on the belief in the legitimacy of an authority that "has always existed."[3] The leader exercising power enjoys authority by virtue of his inherited status. His commands are legitimate in the sense that they are in accordance with customs.[4] Legal domination, on the other hand, consists of a set of rules that are applied judicially and administratively to all members of society in accordance with clearly defined principles. The leaders are elected by legally sanctioned procedures and are themselves subject to the law.

The belief of the followers in the legitimacy of their leader is supported by the latter's ability to satisfy the needs of their society.[5] "Every system of domination," Max Weber observed, "will change its character when its rulers fail to live up to the standards by which they justify their domination and thereby jeopardize the beliefs in those standards among the public at large."[6] Under legal domination, for example, the ruler himself is subject to the law, but he may undermine the beliefs sustaining the legal order if he uses the law to extend his authority.

The predominance of one or another tendency of legitimation is determined by the type of historical configurations existing in society.

In pursuance of their material and ideal interests, rulers may emphasize the type of legitimacy that is best suited to the existing situation. A leader may, for example, emphasize the traditional base of his legitimacy over the legal one to accommodate changing circumstances.

Weber's ideal types are useful to an understanding of the shift in forms of political domination experienced in modern Saudi Arabia. In the process of shaping the political system and its territorial base, Ibn Saud invoked a legitimacy based on a combination of charismatic and traditional elements.[7] He utilized his charisma to mobilize the bedouins and invoked his family's traditional domination of the area and ties to Wahhabism to justify his conquests and the consolidation of his power. As the territorial development of the country neared completion, Ibn Saud created modern administrative structures to meet the demands of a modern nation state. The new pattern of authority that evolved in the late 1920s and early 1930s corresponds to what Weber termed "patrimonial rule."

In his study of traditional authority Weber suggested the existence of two types, which he labeled patriarchal and patrimonial systems.[8] The patriarchal system constitutes the core of all traditional systems and is generally found in household kinship groups in which the head of the household

> has no administrative staff and no machinery to enforce his will. . . .
> The members of the household stand in an entirely personal relation
> to him. They obey him and he commands them in the belief that his
> right and their duty are part of an inviolable order that has the sanctity
> of immemorial tradition.[9]

The patrimonial system displays a different attribute, one in which an identifiable administrative structure develops and spreads throughout society. The tasks of government in this latter system become more specialized, complex, and elaborate. As a result of the specialization of roles and complexity of institutions, the ruler's relationship to the ruled is conducted through a network of bureaucrats. Although differences between the patriarchal and patrimonial system are well marked, the patrimonial form of rule remains an extension of the patriarchal system. Accordingly, Reinhard Bendix defines patrimonial rule as "an extension of the ruler's household in which the relation between the ruler and his officials remains on the basis of paternal authority and filial dependence."[10]

> Under the patrimonial system, the ruler treats all political administration
> as his personal affair, in the same way in which he exploits his possession

of political power as a useful adjunct of his private property. He empowers his officials from case to case, selecting them and assigning them specific tasks on the basis of his personal confidence in them and without establishing any consistent division of labor among them. The officials in turn treat their administrative work for the ruler as a personal service based on their duty of obedience and respect. . . . In their relations with the subject population they can act as arbitrarily as the ruler acts towards them, provided that they do not violate tradition and the interest of the ruler in maintaining the obedience and productive capacity of his subjects.[11]

The personal dimension of patrimonial leadership manifests itself in what Manfred Halpern has described as a "relationship of emanation."[12] The politics of emanation involves an "encounter in which one treats the other solely as an extension of one's self."[13] In brief, then, the leader in a patrimonial system is the center and source of authority. He is "the model, the guide, the innovator, the planner, the mediator, the chastiser, and the protector."[14] Although he may develop a complex administrative structure to assist him in the implementation of policies, the leader remains the center of power.

The questions to be addressed in this part are as follows: (1) What strategy did Saudi rulers adopt in their use of religion and the religious establishment to create the Saudi state and to consolidate their rule? (2) What was the position of the ulama toward the political authority that was instituted? (3) What was the outcome of the interaction between the political authority and the ulama? (4) What changes did Saudi rulers introduce to the pattern of legitimacy as a result of the discovery of oil? (5) What administrative institutions did they establish? (6) How do these institutions function in a patrimonial society? (7) What is the position of the ulama in the new structures? (8) How did the ulama react to changes in Saudi laws? (9) In what areas are they the most/least influential? (10) What policies did Saudi rulers introduce and with what objectives in mind? (11) How did the ulama react to these policies? Finally, (12) what are the future prospects of the existing process of interaction between the ulama, the state, and society at large?

Religion as an Instrument of Expansion and Control

The recapture of Riyadh by Ibn Saud in 1902 marked the beginning of the territorial shaping of the modern Kingdom of Saudi Arabia. In his attempt to expand and consolidate his rule, Ibn Saud revived Wahhabism as a state ideology, stressed the traditional right of his family to rule the area, and used his charisma to buttress his claims. In employing religion and the religious establishment to enhance his political objectives, Ibn Saud adopted a two-pronged policy. On the one hand, he founded and promoted religiously inspired institutions that provided him with general support; created group consciousness; and promoted a common identity that cut across ascriptive ties, offered symbols that linked society to the Saudi family, provided an organizational network to control and direct society, and offered the ruler a loyal fighting force that enabled him to expand his rule. On the other hand, he prevented these institutions from constituting independent centers of power lest they challenge his authority in the future. The political structures and relationships that evolved shattered the hopes of the religious establishment to keep the king united to them by a common cause in return for maintaining their autonomy in the determination and transmission of values and dogma to the populace.

The Territorial Shaping of Modern Saudi Arabia

Apart from Rashidi Najd, the Arabian Peninsula was divided before Ibn Saud's conquest of Riyadh in 1902 into six regions: (1) the Hejaz, extending along the western coast of Arabia on the Red Sea, which was ruled by the sherif of Mecca and formed part of the Ottoman domain; (2) Asir, on the Red Sea between Hejaz and Yemen, which was ruled by the Idressi dynasty and was also part of the Ottoman domain; (3) Northern Arabia, ruled by the Rashid dynasty of Ha'il, which formed a tributary to the Ottoman empire; (4) Hasa, along the Gulf between Kuwait and the Trucial Coast, which was a province of the Ottoman empire; (5) Yemen, under the Zaidi imams of San'a, which formed part of the Ottoman empire; and (6) the Gulf and South Arabian principalities, sultanates, and shaykhdoms, which included Kuwait, Bahrain, Qatar, the Trucial Coast, Muscat and Oman, Hadhramout, and Aden, and which were all under British protection. Of these territories, only Yemen and the British protected areas did not eventually fall under Saudi rule.[1]

When Ibn Saud was about twenty-two years old, he marched on Riyadh with forty men and defeated the Rashidi garrison on January 12, 1902. Ibn Rashid was preparing to attack Kuwait, in an attempt to annex it to his domain, when he received the news of the fall of Riyadh and the death of his governor, Ajlan, at the hands of Ibn Saud. He refrained from taking action against Ibn Saud, however, because he believed that it was within his power to recapture Riyadh at any time he wished. Taking advantage of Ibn Rashid's inaction, Ibn Saud began to fortify his position in the city. To enhance his legitimacy among the city's inhabitants and devote his time to expanding Saudi rule, Ibn Saud entrusted his father, Imam Abd al-Rahman, with the administration of Riyadh.

One town after another fell under Saudi attack. By the spring of 1904, Ibn Saud had become the ruler of central Najd and had pushed his boundaries to the confines of Jabal Shammar. The Ottomans were apprehensive of Ibn Saud and the spread of his domain. Subsequently, they increased their support to the Rashidis, but the Saudi forces were able to continue their push to control the peninsula.[2]

By 1913, the Ottomans were unable to restrain the expansion of the Saudi state. The Ottoman empire was engaged in war with Italy over the possession of Libya as well as certain Mediterranean islands, thus allowing Ibn Saud to annex the Hasa region. Ibn Saud's position was further strengthened when the British government concluded a treaty with him in 1914 recognizing Najd, Hasa, Qatif, and Jubail and its dependencies as part of the Saudi domain. During the war, Ibn Saud aided the Allies' war effort by avoiding military action against Sherif Hussein, ruler of the Hejaz and supporter of the British. However, continued British support to Sherif Hussein in the years that followed World War I led Ibn Saud to devise plans to conquer the Hejaz. The British had already installed Hussein's two sons, Faisal and Abd Allah, as rulers of British-dominated Iraq and Transjordan, respectively. Moreover, in 1924, Sherif Hussein proclaimed himself "Caliph of the Muslims" in addition to his previous title, "King of the Arabs."

Realizing the urgency surrounding the conquest of Hejaz, Ibn Saud called the ulama of Riyadh and the tribal leaders under the Saudi domain on June 2, 1924, to a conference and stated that "it is time to put an end to the follies of him who calls himself the Sherif of Mecca. Never in the history of Islam has a man so corrupt dared to clothe himself with the dignity of Caliph."[3] A few months later, a Saudi force consisting of 3,000 warriors set out for Ta'if and captured it after slaughtering its Hashemite garrison. The news of how Ibn Saud's army massacred the Ta'if garrison reached Jeddah. Fearing for their lives, the city's merchants and ulama deposed King Hussein and installed in his stead Amir Ali, Hussein's son. But Ali had little time to exercise any authority. The forces of Ibn Saud occupied Jeddah and the holy cities of Mecca and Medina in 1926; in the same year, Ibn Saud proclaimed himself king of Hejaz. Six years later, Ibn Saud was proclaimed king of the Kingdom of Saudi Arabia.

The Consolidation of Saudi Rule: Legitimation of Rule Through the Ulama

Ibn Saud's charisma and his use of the Wahhabi ideology proved to be extremely helpful tools in the conquest of the Arabian Peninsula and the consolidation of his rule throughout the newly conquered territories. As leader, Ibn Saud alluded to the mission he was called upon to perform. His advocacy of a revivalist movement in search of lost glory supplemented this charismatic authority and capitalized on his family's traditional association with Al Shaykh and Wahhabism.

Ibn Saud's personality enabled him to galvanize the bedouins to action; his knowledge of and aptitude for desert warfare and the handling of bedouins led to victories. Success gave his claims additional legitimacy and furthered his charisma in the eyes of his followers. Ibn Saud used his knowledge of the history of the area and of the workings of its society to justify his conquests and to consolidate his position among the tribes of the peninsula and the area's urban inhabitants in both historical and religious terms. Dankwart Rustow tells us that "if a leader is to be a major innovator, [he needs] a particular attitude toward the recent and the more distant past of his society."[4] To the outstanding leader, "the remote past may become a powerful ally against the immediate past for a better future."[5] Indeed, Ibn Saud was well aware of his family's history, the vicissitudes of his people, the psychology of the urban and bedouin inhabitants of the peninsula, and the difficulty of controlling the bedouins. It was to expand his rule and consolidate his authority that Ibn Saud deliberately set out in his revival of Wahhabism to destroy the tribal organization and create in its place a sense of national cohesion.

It was not too long, however, before the ideals of Wahhabism were shattered under the impact of political reality and the demands of modern social and political organization. Ibn Saud realized the need for modern vehicles in order to facilitate the transport of pilgrims to the holy places and to mechanize his army, but the ulama objected in principle to any changes. Similarly, while Ibn Saud aspired to modify the country's laws and administrative institutions, the ulama insisted that answers to contemporary situations be sought in the *shari'ah* and traditional Islamic institutions.

Ibn Saud's position vis-à-vis Wahhabism and his relations with the ulama were determined by his political objectives and the type of social and historical configurations that existed. As for the ulama themselves, their general position toward political authority was endorsement and support of policies that did not contradict Wahhabi principles and that limited opposition to those policies they viewed as un-Islamic. To understand the factors contributing to the ulama's docile position with respect to Ibn Saud, it is necessary to examine the structure and composition of the ulama establishment in Saudi society.

Najdi and Hejazi Ulama: Composition and Background

Generally speaking, the ulama may be defined as those theological and legal experts who through their personal conduct and knowledge gained the respect and recognition of the community in general and the political authorities in particular. Accordingly, in Najd ulama were present in urban centers, small towns, and villages, as well as in bedouin settlements. Existing at no time, however, was a structured religious hierarchy similar to the Egyptian ulama, for example. Despite the absence of a hierarchical organization, Najdi ulama were differentiated according to a set of informal criteria. Among their ranks, some were recognized by their colleagues as more learned, and Al Saud sought their advice and support. H. St. John Philby noted in 1918, for example, that the leading ulama consisted of "six at Riyadh, three in the Qasim, a similar number in the Hasa, and one in each of the other districts or provinces of Najd—some twenty or more in all."[6] The number of the leading ulama was not the same at all times. Some *fatwas* (religious proclamations) contained the names of fifteen ulama, while others had more or fewer names. It is certain, however, that the Riyadh ulama enjoyed a position of preeminence among their colleagues. This preeminent position may be attributed to their presence in the capital and their proximity to the ruler.

Another group that enjoyed a privileged position among the ulama were the descendants of Shaykh Muhammad Ibn Abd al-Wahhab. This group supported Saudi rule and identified its survival and fortunes with their own. As indicated in Table 3.1, Abd Allah Ibn Shaykh Muhammad, for example, served three Saudi rulers. He accompanied Imam Saud in his conquest of Mecca in 1803 and authored pamphlets and tracts propagating Wahhabi principles. His son, Sulayman Ibn Shaykh Abd Allah, was appointed judge of Mecca by Imam Saud in 1810. He endorsed Saudi rule of the holy cities and condemned all opponents of Saudi rule as infidels.

In brief, then, Al Shaykh justified the policies of Al Saud by authoring pamphlets and texts that amplified Wahhabi doctrines, by acting as judges and administrators in conquered areas, and more important by identifying the rule of Al Saud with Wahhabism. Because of their close identification with Al Saud, the fate of Al Shaykh was determined by the wishes of Al Saud and by the fate of Al Saud themselves. For example, Abd al-Rahman Al Shaykh was appointed by Imam Abd Allah as judge of Dar'iya. When the forces of Muhammad Ali attacked the city in 1818, Abd al-Rahman accompanied Imam Abd Allah in battle against the Egyptian army and was subsequently taken hostage to Egypt. When Turki Ibn Abd Allah Ibn Muhammad Al Saud recaptured Najd from the Egyptians in 1824, Abd al-Rahman escaped from Egypt and returned to Najd the following year. He was appointed mufti of Riyadh, for Dar'iya had been razed to the ground by the Egyptians. In his new post, he provided Imam Turki with the religious legitimacy he needed to justify his rule and authored a number of pamphlets propagating Wahhabism.

Abd al-Rahman's son, Shaykh Abd al-Latif, followed more or less the same pattern as that of his father in his relationship with Al Saud. When the Rashidis attacked Riyadh in 1890, Abd al-Latif was taken hostage to Ha'il, the Rashidi capital. He was allowed to return to Riyadh a year later, provided that he confined his activities to religious instruction. When Ibn Saud conquered Riyadh in 1902, however, Abd al-Latif became instrumental in providing Ibn Saud with the religious sanction and support he needed to legitimate his regime. To symbolize the durability of the alliance between the Saudi family and Al Shaykh, Ibn Saud married Shaykh Abd al-Latif's daughter.

The ulama of Hejaz differed from their Najdi counterparts in social background, education, and outlook. These differences were influenced by the disparities in the social and political settings between the two regions. Whereas Najdi society was mostly tribal and subject to almost no foreign influence at all, Hejaz was urban in its politics and outlook, its power was concentrated in the cities of Mecca, Medina, and Jedda,

TABLE 3.1
The Religious Elite: Al Shaykh*

Name	Date and Place of Birth	Children	Education	Career	Relation with Al Saud
Shaykh Muhammad Ibn Abd al-Wahhab	b. 1704 in Najd	Ali, Hussein, Abd Allah, Hassan, Ibrahim, Abd al-Aziz**	Was tutored in Hanbali jurisprudence by his father.	Co-founder of the first Saudi State.	Co-ruled the first Saudi State.
Abd Allah Ibn Shaykh Muhammad Ibn Abd al-Wahhab	b. 1751; d. 1856; Dar'iya	Sulayman, Abd al-Rahman	Was tutored in the principles of Wahhabism by his father.	Succeeded his father as propagator of Wahhabism, Chief Mufti, and head of the judicial system.	Served under three Saudi rulers: Imam Abd al-Aziz, Imam Saud, Imam Abd Allah. Accompanied Imam Saud in the conquest of Mecca. Authored pamphlets propagating Wahhabism and rejecting Zaidi Shi'ism.
Sulayman Ibn Shaykh Abd Allah	b. 1785; d. 1817; Dar'iya	No children	Was tutored in the principles of Wahhabism by his father.	Lectured principles of Wahhabism in Dar'iya. Was appointed by Imam Saud as Judge of Mecca.	Supported Saudi rule. Urged the Imam not to deal with infidels (i.e., all non-Wahhabis).

*Information on Al Shaykh is derived from Abd al-Rahman Ibn Abd al-Latif Ibn Abd Allah Ibn Abd al-Latif al Shaykh, Ulama' al-Da'wa (Cairo: Midani Press, 1966).

**Ali, Hussein, Abd Allah, and Hassan became leading ulama. Ibrahim and Abd al-Aziz had no children.

TABLE 3.1 (cont.)

Name	Date and Place of Birth	Children	Education	Career	Relation with Al Saud
Abd al-Rahman Ibn Hassan	b. 1779; d. 1868; Dar'iya.	Muhammad, Abd al-Latif, Abd Allah, Isma'il.*	Was tutored in the principles of Wahhabism by his grandfather, Shaykh Muhammad.**	Became judge of Dar'iya. Lectured Wahhabism. After his return from Egypt, became Mufti of Riyadh.	Accompanied Imam Abd Allah in battle against Egyptian forces. Was taken hostage with his son Abd al-Latif to Egypt. When Turki Ibn Abd Allah Ibn Muhammad Al Saud recaptured Najd from the Egyptians, he returned to the area in 1852 and provided Imam Turki the support he needed to consolidate his rule. Authored a number of books propagating Wahhabism.
Abd al-Latif Ibn al-Shaykh Abd al-Rahman	b. 1848; d. (?); Dar'iya.	No information	Was tutored in the principles of Wahhabism by his father.	Lectured in Ha'il. Became Chief Mufti of Riyadh during the reign of Ibn Saud. Organized the Mutawi'a.	When the Rashidis attacked Riyadh in 1890, he was taken hostage to Ha'il. The Rashidis allowed him to return to Riyadh in 1891. Following Ibn Saud's conquest of Riyadh in 1901, he endorsed Saudi rule. Ibn Saud renewed the alliance between Al Saud and Al Shaykh by marrying Abd al-Latif's daughter, mother of King Faisal.

*Abd al-Latif and Ishaq became leading ulama.

**He in turn tutored four members of the family: Abd al-Malik Ibn Hussein Ibn Muhammad, Abd al-Rahman Ibn Hussein Ibn Muhammad, Hussein Ibn Hassan Ibn Hussein, and Abd al-Aziz Ibn Muhammad Ibn Ali Muhammad. All four became leading ulama.

46

TABLE 3.1 (cont.)

Name	Date and Place of Birth	Children	Education	Career	Relation with Al Saud
Abd Allah Ibn Hassan Ibn Hussein Ibn Ali Ibn Hussein Ibn Abd al-Wahhab	b. 1870, Riyadh; d. (?)	Muhammad,* Abd al-Aziz, Hassan,** Ibrahim, Ahmad***	Was tutored by his father in the principles of Wahhabism and Islamic sciences.	Imam of Riyadh Mosque.*** Was sent by Ibn Saud to instruct the Ikhwan of Artawiya in the principles of Wahhabism. Became Qadi in Ibn Saud's army. Was appointed by Ibn Saud Imam and Khatib of the Mecca Mosque. Became Chief Qadi of Hejaz and controller and supervisor of Holy Places in Mecca and Medina. Supervised religious education in the Mecca and Medina mosques.	Supported and advocated Ibn Saud's policies among the ulama and the Ikhwan.

*He also oversaw the education of the ulama as well as of many members of his family, including Salih Ibn Abd al-Aziz Ibn Abd al-Rahman Ibn Hussein, future Mufti of the state; Abd al-Latif Ibn Ibrahim Ibn Abd al-Latif; Omar Ibn Hassan, future head of the Committees for Commanding the Good and Forbidding the Evil in the Central and Eastern Provinces; and Abd Allah Ibn Hassan, future Chief Judge of the Hejaz region.

**No children.

***Became a leading alem.

TABLE 3.1 (cont.)

Name	Date and Place of Birth	Children	Education	Career	Relation with Al Saud
Muhammad Ibn Abd Allah Ibn Hassan Ibn Hussein Ibn Ali Ibn Hussein Ibn Abd al-Wahhab	No information	No information	Was tutored in the principles of Wahhabism by his father.	Director of religious affairs, Western Province.	Supported the rule of Al Saud.
Abd al-Aziz Ibn Abd Allah Ibn Hassan Ibn Hussein Ibn Ali Ibn Hussein Ibn Abd al-Wahhab	No information	No information	Was tutored in the principles of Wahhabism by his father.	Minister of Education; Khatib at the Mecca Mosque.	Supported the rule of Al Saud.
Hassan Ibn Abd Allah Ibn Hassan Ibn Hussein Ibn Ali Ibn Hussein Ibn Abd al-Wahhab	No information	No information	Was tutored in the principles of Wahhabism by his father.	Minister of higher Education.	Supported the rule of Al Saud.

and it had always been subject to the influence of cultures external to the peninsula. Economically, Hejaz was prosperous in comparison with Ibn Saud's impoverished Najd. Yearly, pilgrims to the holy cities constituted the primary source of wealth in Hejaz, and the pilgrimages served as a means of cultural contact with the outside world. Because of this cultural richness, Hejazis, including their ulama, were less rigid in their social outlook and less austere in their daily lives than were their counterparts in Najd.

S. C. Snouck Hurgronje identified Hejazi ulama as those who specialized in *fiqh* (jurisprudence), *Quranic* exegesis, Traditions, Arabic grammar, syntax, prosody, logic, and philosophy.[7] The region's leading ulama were mostly Azhar graduates or those who studied in the Mecca and Medina mosques. Najdi ulama, on the other hand, had concentrated in their learning as well as in their teaching on the principles of Wahhabism and Hanbali *fiqh,* with little interest in grammar, syntax, or other traditional subjects of Islamic sciences. Moreover, the religious education of Al Shaykh was handed down from father to son, with little contact with outside scholars. Shaykh Muhammad Ibn Abd al-Wahhab instructed his son Abd Allah, who in turn instructed his son Sulayman. Shaykh Abd al-Rahman Ibn Hassan was tutored by his grandfather, Shaykh Muhammad. He in turn instructed his son Shaykh Abd al-Latif Ibn al-Shaykh Abd al-Rahman.[8] The difference in educational background between the Najdi and Hejazi ulama made the former more fanatical and literal in their understanding and application of religion. It was therefore not surprising that whereas the Najdi ulama opposed the introduction of any innovation, their Hejazi counterparts were more willing to depart from tradition.

Notwithstanding the differences between the two groups of ulama, both depended on political authority for survival. As with the Najdi ulama who drew their salaries from the state, many Hejazi ulama received salaries from their political benefactors. Others survived on donations, pilgrims' gifts, and *awqaf* revenues or engaged in commerce. Those receiving salaries from the political authority in Hejaz were viewed by their colleagues and the population in general as most prominent. This fact may be attributed to their proximity to political authority and, hence, their greater influence.

Whereas some Hejazi ulama survived on donations, gifts, or *awqaf* revenues and enjoyed relative autonomy in the conduct of their daily affairs, Najdi ulama were totally dependent for their material existence on state subsidies. The dependence of Najdi ulama on state financial support arose from the principles of Wahhabism itself, which prohibit the ulama from receiving gifts and donations or surviving on *awqaf* revenues.

Although Najdi ulama supported the cause of Al Saud, leading Hejazi ulama took it upon themselves to defend the authority of their rulers. Ibn Ghanam recorded a debate that took place between Najdi and Hejazi ulama during the reign of Sherif Ghalib (1788–1813). In an attempt to refute Wahhabism, the leading ulama of Mecca criticized their Najdi counterparts for declaring non-Wahhabi Muslims to be infidels.[9] By focusing on this issue, the Mecca ulama did not challenge the tenets of Wahhabism so much as reject Wahhabi denunciation of other Muslims as infidels. In other words, the Meccan ulama attempted to convince their Najdi counterparts that to fight other Muslims, including their own amir of Mecca, was un-Islamic. According to them, the amir of Mecca is a Muslim ruler who applies the *shari'ah*, and his authority should be accepted.

Following Ibn Saud's conquest of Hejaz, the region's ulama submitted to Saudi rule. Their leaders issued a *fatwa* sanctioning Ibn Saud's take-over of the holy places and urged all Muslims to obey the new ruler.

In addition to their role as legitimators of political authority, both Najdi and Hejazi ulama acted as mediators between the rulers and their subjects. Given their proximity to political authority, the ulama's conduct played a crucial role in the process by which social communication was carried on and thus contributed to the integration of society into a working whole.[10] For instance, Shaykh Ahmad Zayni Dahlan, the mufti of Mecca, was the religious leader through whom the Ottomans legitimated their policies in the area. In addition to issuing the appropriate *fatwas* required of him, Dahlan was authorized to appoint professors and instructors in the Mecca mosque, to supervise the educational system in the city's mosques, and to look after the affairs of the ulama in general. Informally, he was the mediator between the merchants and the authority, the rich and the poor, the ruler and the ruled.

Although Najdi ulama were generally supportive of Saudi rule, their relations with Ibn Saud were far from harmonious. For example, in 1925 the Riyadh ulama issued a *fatwa* calling on Ibn Saud to refuse the Shi'is of Hasa the right to worship publicly; to force them to appear before ulama representatives and submit to the "religion of God and His Prophet"; to compel them to cease calling upon members of the House of the Prophet, including Ali and his sons Hassan and Hussein; to halt their celebrations on the anniversaries of the birth and death of Muhammad and Ali; to prevent them from visiting Karbala and Najaf; to force them to attend the five prayers in mosques; to compel them to undergo instruction in the writings of Shaykh

Muhammad Ibn Abd al-Wahhab; and to destroy Shi'i worship places in the Hasa.

Ruling by the strength of his personality and by force and coercion, Ibn Saud rejected the ulama's *fatwa*. Instead, he taxed the Shi'is for the protection he granted them. Ibn Saud's rejection of ulama demands was not limited to this incident. Indeed, as H. C. Armstrong has noted, "in matters of religion [Ibn Saud] submitted to the wishes of the ulama, but when they rendered him advice on political or military matters, with which he disagreed, he sent them back to their books."[11] In June 1930, the ulama met in Mecca to discuss Ibn Saud's educational policies. They issued a *fatwa* protesting the inclusion of foreign languages, geography, and drawing in the curricula of the newly founded Directorate of Education. They objected to the study of foreign languages because they believed that this would enable Muslims to learn the religion of unbelievers; to geography because it presupposed that the earth is round, while a *Quranic* verse indicates that it is flat; and to drawing because, with painting, it reproduces God's Creation. Ibn Saud was not inclined to eliminate these subjects. He was determined to create, in addition to the already existing *Quranic* schools, a modern educational system. He informed the ulama that their *fatwa* demonstrated ignorance of Islam, which urges believers to acquire knowledge, and asked Hafiz Wahbah, the head of the newly founded directorate, to include all three subjects in the curriculum.

In summary, Ibn Saud's attitude toward the ulama was influenced by his political objectives. On the one hand, he sought ulama support and endorsement of his rule; on the other, he rejected their traditional right to judge and evaluate the ruler's policies. Although the ulama identified themselves with Saudi authority, they disagreed with many of its policies. They expressed their disagreement through the issuance of *fatwa*s and in private audiences with the king. Because of their close relation with all strata of the population (through public prayers as well as the Friday sermon) and their control of the traditional educational system, the ulama could have mobilized the masses against Ibn Saud's authority. However, it appears that they adopted a passive attitude toward political authority and continued to hope that the king's policy would express Wahhabi principles.

The Creation and Subsequent Subjugation of the Ikhwan

Whereas the ulama provided Ibn Saud with the religious legitimation he needed to consolidate his rule, Wahhabi ideology was instrumental in mobilizing the bedouin society to expand Saudi domain. With the restoration of Saudi rule in Najd, Ibn Saud realized that no central authority and modern political structure could be established in an unstable tribal society. The majority of the peninsula's population was tribal, consisting of people who mistrusted and rejected any central authority because of their fear of taxation, military conscription, and the general loss of autonomy. The eclipse of the Saudi state in the 1800s permitted the bedouin to revert to the intertribal feuding and superstitious practices that Ibn Abd al-Wahhab thought he had obliterated. Based on his understanding of bedouin society, Ibn Saud realized that the bedouin could become a powerful fighting force if the means could be found to motivate them. Wahhabism became the ideology, *jihad* became the instrument, and the Ikhwan were Ibn Saud's warriors.

Describing the genesis of the Ikhwan, Hafiz Wahbah wrote:

> Wahhabi teaching was formerly preached amongst town-dwellers only. Consequently, Bedouins were responsible to a great extent for much of the upheaval that had taken place at different times. They always sided with the party whom they dreaded most or who promised them most booty. That is why they were sometimes counted as Egyptians or Turkish or Wahhabis or Rashidites. The onus of defence fell thereby on the shoulders of town-dwellers. King Ibn Saud thought fit to tackle this Bedouin question by establishing special dwellings for them to follow agricultural pursuits, . . . and whereas they were formerly a danger to whichever party they elected to support, they have now become staunch and reliable in the face of death itself.[12]

In creating the settlements, Ibn Saud deliberately emphasized a militant Wahhabi spirit among the bedouins. The belief system that rationalized and inspired the Ikhwan movement was developed by Shaykh Abd Allah Ibn Muhammad Ibn Abd al-Latif Al Shaykh. He amplified Wahhabi principles to coincide with Ibn Saud's political objectives and organized a network of religious instructors who propagated these principles. Above all, his writings emphasized the dual duty to obey God and the Imam. They also stressed the evils of innovation and the religious obligation of believers to fight infidels.

To indoctrinate the bedouins, instructors were sent to the tribes with the message that "Islam is a sedentary religion" (*al-Islam din hadari*).[13] Moreover, Ibn Saud summoned tribal shaykhs to Riyadh and told them

> in blunt terms that [their] tribe had no religion and that they were all 'juhal' [ignorant of Islam]. He next ordered the [shaykhs] to attend the local school of ulama which was attached to the great mosque in Riyadh,

and there undergo a course of instruction in religion. At the same time half a dozen ulama, attended by some genuinely fanatical [I] khwan . . . were sent off to the tribe itself. These held daily classes teaching the people all about Islam in its original simplicity. . . . When the Shaykh of the tribe was supposed to have received sufficient religious instruction, he was invited to build a house in Riyadh and remain in attendance on the imam. This again was part of the control scheme.[14]

Linked closely to the notion of Jahlliyah (ignorance of Islam) was the concept of *hijrah* (migration). In emulation of the Prophet's flight to Medina, which led to the creation of the first Islamic community, the ideology of the Ikhwan viewed migration from the land of polytheism to the land of Islam as a duty incumbent upon all Muslims. In *Thalathat al-Usul,* Shaykh Muhammad Ibn Abd al-Wahhab cited the following *Quranic* verses to urge believers to migrate from the land of *shirk* (polytheism) to the land of Islam:

Lo! as for those whom the angels ask: in what were you engaged? They will say: we were oppressed in the land. [The angels] will say: was not Allah's earth spacious that you could have migrated therein? As for such, their habitation will be hell, an evil journey's end; . . . Who so migrateth for the cause of Allah will find much refuge and abundance in the earth, and whose forsaketh his home, a fugitive unto Allah and His messenger, and death overtaketh him, his reward is then incumbent on Allah.[15]

The Structure and Organization of Ikhwan Settlements

The first Ikhwan settlement was founded in December 1912 at al-Artawiya, an area that possessed good pasture land and wells. This area was within the domain (*dira*) of the Mutayr tribe. Certainly, were Ibn Saud to succeed in leading this tribe to give up its tribal nature, his accomplishment would come to be regarded as a remarkable one. It was a tribe known for its warlike traits, its frequent raids against neighboring areas, and its rejection of central authority. Through skillful use of force and indoctrination, Ibn Saud settled this tribe along with a subgroup of the Harb tribe, thus weakening tribal ties and promoting relations based on a subscription to a common ideology.

Two hundred and twenty other settlements followed the experiment that began at al-Artawiya.[16] The majority of these settlements were founded in Najd and on the fringes of the Hejaz and the Saudi-Transjordanian borders. The broad geographical distribution of these settlements in the region made Ibn Saud's physical presence felt across the peninsula and provided him with military bases, supply bases, and religious outposts.[17]

In a record of his travels to the peninsula, Amin al-Rihani remarked that the population of the *hujar* (settlements) was divided into three groups: (1) the bedouin who had become farmers, (2) the *mutawi'a*, and (3) merchants and craftsmen.[18] The distinction between the farmers and the merchant-craftsmen group was tribal in origin. Members of noble tribes became agriculturalists, whereas those of ignoble origin functioned as merchants and tradesmen.[19] Despite Ikhwan assertions that theirs was a community of equals, members of ignoble tribes did not participate in *ghazw* (raids); they remained in the settlement, performing such necessary services as shoeing horses, making swords and spears, and repairing weapons and utensils.[20]

It is not exactly clear which social elements made up the *mutawi'a*, who were under the direct control of the Riyadh ulama and were normally recruited from outside the tribal units of the settlement. Each *mutawi'*, however, had a *tilmidh* (a *mutawi'* trainee) who was recruited from the local settlement. The *mutawi'a* did not enjoy any administrative or judicial functions. Rather, they distributed themselves usually in a ratio of one to fifty among members of the settlements and conducted sessions of religious instruction. They also enforced the general principles of Wahhabism.

Each settlement was governed by an amir and a *hakim* (administrator).[21] The amir was responsible for the implementation of administrative decrees emanating from the Consultative Council in Riyadh (*majlis al-shura*). This council was composed of Mufti Abd Allah Al Shaykh, the leading ulama, tribal leaders, and some urban notables. Council decisions became effective only after ratification by Ibn Saud, who held the title of President of the Council. The *hakim*, on the other hand, was responsible for the general application of the dictates of the *shari'ah*. In addition to the amir and the *hakim*, each settlement had a *qadi* (judge), who was appointed by Ibn Saud. The majority of *qadis* were drawn from Al-Shaykh's family.[22]

The Ikhwan as a Military Force

Daily life in the settlements was dedicated to prayer, study of *al-tawhid*, cultivation of land, and constant preparation for war. The Ikhwan viewed the world and its inhabitants in term of believers (i.e., the Ikhwan themselves) and nonbelievers. All nonbelievers should be converted by the sword, they maintained. This vision of the world and its inhabitants served Ibn Saud's interest in justifying the expansion of his domain. To accomplish the objective of territorial expansion, he divided the inhabitants of each settlement into three classes: (1) those personnel in a state of semi-alert who responded to the first call of *jihad;* (2) the reserve forces, composed of herdsmen and tradesmen; and (3) all those who remained in the settlement to maintain daily business. Ibn Saud had the right to call up the first and second groups, whereas the ulama's approval was needed to mobilize the third.[23]

The Ikhwan's first appearance as a military force in the battle of Jirab in 1914 had radically altered the balance of power in the area. In the Hejaz, Sherif Hussein relied militarily on an urban-regular army, trained by the Ottomans and the British and provided by the Syrians and the Iraqis with officers. This army, however, lacked the Ikhwan's dedication to their cause and the mobility of the bedouins.[24] The Ottoman-equipped Rashidi army was composed mostly of the Shammar tribe, whose allegiance to the Rashidi cause was based on convenience rather than ideological commitment. The Ikhwan, on the other hand, considered themselves the guardians of state security and morals. Their increased political and military power created among their ranks a group consciousness that did not exist among the forces of Sherif Hussein or the Rashidis. They were highly mobile and well trained in desert warfare.

Schooled in the notion that Wahhabism is the only path for Muslims to follow, the Ikhwan were able to win for Ibn Saud every battle in which they were engaged between 1914 and 1927. He was their Imam, and Wahhabism was their cause. In the conquest of Hejaz, the Ikhwan leaders as well as the ulama, tribal shaykhs, and urban notables were called to a conference in Riyadh on June 5, 1924. Ibn Saud informed them that the Ikhwan had expressed their desire to make the pilgrimage to Mecca and Medina, but Sherif Hussein prevented them from performing this religious duty. After presenting his position, Ibn Saud requested the ulama's *fatwa* concerning the validity of waging war to guarantee the right of believers to perform their religious duty. The ulama supported Ibn Saud's position, and their *fatwa* was in reality an order to the Ikhwan to wage war against Sherif Hussein. Four thousand Ikhwan, all dressed as pilgrims carrying arms, attacked Ta'if. They massacred its garrison and systematically destroyed everything they viewed as contravening Wahhabi principles. Following Ta'if, Mecca fell under Ikhwan control, and strict observance of Wahhabism was enforced.

The End of Wahhabi Fanaticism and the Assertion of Moderation: The Subjugation of the Ikhwan

With the conquest of the Hejaz, Ibn Saud's territorial shaping of the kingdom was completed. He no longer needed the Ikhwan as a fighting force, and their religious fanaticism became a potential threat to his regime. Ibn Saud had fired the Ikhwan into a fanatical and uncompromising force precisely because that was what he needed. Having accomplished his political objective, he needed to diffuse the Ikhwan fanaticism. The Riyadh ulama recalled their *mutawi'a* from the Ikhwan settlements and instructed them to preach that Islam is the religion of the middle road (*al-Islam din wassat*) and that Islam is not opposed to material comfort and wealth. The implications of the new dogma were twofold: First, the Ikhwan were expected to shun their religious fanaticism; second, the Ikhwan were to devote their time and resources to the cultivation of the land and the acquisition of wealth.

The Ikhwan rejected the moderate interpretation of Islam. They claimed *jihad* against Transjordan, Iraq, and Kuwait. It was their leader's dealing with the British, however, that angered them and escalated their conflict with Ibn Saud. The first indication of the gravity of the situation surfaced in 1925, in Mecca. Over five months had elapsed since the Ikhwan had conquered this city, but Ibn Saud refused their request to advance to Jeddah and Medina, a task that was easily within their reach. He felt that a negotiated surrender might be secured from the leaders of Medina and Jedda, but the Ikhwan insisted that conversion by the sword was the only way. On April 24, 1925, Faisal al-Duwaish, an Ikhwan leader, warned Ibn Saud that the swords of his warriors were prepared to deal with those who might perpetuate the misdeeds of the deposed Sherif Hussein.[25]

Reaffirming their belief in *jihad* as incumbent upon adult male Muslims, the Ikhwan met in December 1926 in al-Artawiya and censured Ibn Saud for not continuing the war against neighboring areas. They also censured their Imam for (1) sending his son Saud to Egypt, a land controlled by the British; (2) sending his son Faisal to London in 1926 to curry favor with the British; (3) introducing into the land of Islam the telegraph, telephone, and automobile, all viewed as instruments of the devil; (4) levying custom taxes on the Muslims in Najd; (5) granting permission to the tribes of Jordan and Iraq to graze their herds in the land of Islam; (6) prohibiting commerce with Kuwait (the Ikhwan informed Ibn Saud that if the people of Kuwait were infidels, then he should wage holy war against them; if they were considered Muslims, then the ruler should not prevent commerce with them); and finally, (7) tolerating the Shi'is of Hasa. The Ikhwan believed that they should be either converted to Wahhabism or killed.[26]

Because of the gravity of the Ikhwan's complaints, the Riyadh ulama found it necessary to explain their position. They issued a *fatwa* adopting a neutral stand on the question of the telegraph, radio, and the automobile but advised the king to follow Wahhabi principles and destroy the Mosque of Hamza, which was a Shi'i shrine; to forbid the entrance of the Egyptian *mahmal* (procession, or parade) into the holy cities of Mecca and Medina; to force the Shi'is to submit to Islam or be expelled from the kingdom; to prevent the Shi'is of Iraq from grazing their herds in the land of Islam; and to return the taxes the government had collected from the inhabitants of Najd. Although the ulama supported the Ikhwan position in their *fatwa*, they insisted that it was the Imam's responsibility alone to declare *jihad*.[27]

Rejecting the *fatwa*'s insistence that the Imam alone has the responsibility to declare *jihad*, the Ikhwan, on November 6, 1927, raided an Iraqi police post near the Saudi border and massacred all its members. They also raided Kuwait as well as Transjordan. To halt further Ikhwan raids, the British government ordered its air force to pursue the Ikhwan raiders across Najd. The situation developed exactly as the Ikhwan leader Faisal al-Duwaish had desired. Ibn Saud could be accused only of religious laxity if he refused to meet the British infidels on the battlefield.

Having completed the territorial shaping of Saudi Arabia, Ibn Saud was not interested in confronting the British or expanding his domain. To harness Ikhwan fanaticism, he called for a general assembly on November 6, 1928, in the city of Riyadh. More than eight hundred Ikhwan attended, as well as the ulama and urban and tribal notables. Ibn Saud addressed the assembly and recounted his religious and political achievements, including his unification of the peninsula. In an attempt to elicit support, Ibn Saud offered his resignation on the condition that the assembly select a successor from Al Saud. As Hafiz Wahbah has noted, no one really believed that Ibn Saud was willing to abdicate. The ulama and notables refused Ibn Saud's offer of resignation and endorsed his rule.

Following the Riyadh conference, the Ikhwan realized that naked force was the only way to depose Ibn Saud. Their leaders spread the word among the settlements that they alone, that is, the Ikhwan, remained the true defenders of Wahhabism. The Ikhwan leaders, Faisal al-Duwaish of the Mutayr tribe, Sultan Ibn Humaid Ibn Bijad of the Utaiba, and Didan Ibn Hithlin of the Ujman, launched a series of military attacks against not only Iraq and Kuwait but also some Najdi tribes that were loyal to Ibn Saud. Ibn Saud and the Ikhwan confronted each other on March 31, 1929, in the battle of Sibila. Ibn Saud's army, composed of urban and rural recruits as well as loyal bedouins, defeated the Ikhwan and asserted Ibn Saud's rule. The settlements were dismantled, and the Ikhwan were converted into the National Guard.

Conclusion

In his attempt to expand Saudi rule and consolidate his authority, Ibn Saud reaffirmed Wahhabism as a state ideology and established religiously inspired institutions to promote and implement his policies. By maintaining the traditional alliance between his family and Al Shaykh, he projected his rule as a continuation of the first Saudi state in which the relationship between religion and state was a harmonious one. Ibn Saud created the Ikhwan and indoctrinated them with militant Wahhabism so as to identify the expansion of his rule with the expansion of Wahhabism.

Although the ulama were generally supportive of Ibn Saud's rule, their relationship with him was far from harmonious. The ulama, as well as the Ikhwan leaders, aspired to keep Ibn Saud united to them by a common cause, but the reality of political life shattered their vision. Ibn Saud needed Wahhabism to legitimate his rule, but innovation was also needed if Saudi Arabia was to keep abreast of the twentieth century. As a result, although Wahhabism continued to be the state ideology, the ulama were stripped of their traditional heritage. Ibn Saud was the source of all authority in the state, and the religious institutions were to act according to his political needs. It was not surprising, therefore, that whereas Ibn Saud established and/or strengthened religious institutions in the earlier stages, he dismantled some of these institutions and restricted the activities of others in the later period. The challenge that confronted Ibn Saud and his successors was to continue the use of Wahhabism as a state ideology while developing a modern state as well.

Expansion of State Control and Incorporation of the Ulama in State Administration

For over two decades, from its proclamation as a unified kingdom in 1932 until 1953, Saudi Arabia survived without any elaborate administrative institutions. During this period, Ibn Saud ruled personally and informally. He administered the country as a gigantic personal household, not allowing power to be concentrated at any point in the system. The expansion of the oil-extracting industry in the 1950s and the subsequent increase in government revenues, however, brought about an increasing complexity in governmental institutions and the expansion of government jurisdiction over a large number of societal areas. The death of Ibn Saud in 1953 was not followed by the disintegration of the state he had founded. Instead, the Saudi state survived its founder's death, and Ibn Saud's successors (Saud, 1953–1964; Faisal, 1964–1975; Khalid, 1975–1982; Fahd, 1982 until the present) have continued to establish modern administrative structures to enhance governmental performance that complement the traditional base of the regime's legitimacy. Indeed, the development of complex and modern administrative institutions has enabled Saudi rulers to control society and maintain their traditional rule.

The creation of complex administrative institutions has led to two fundamental changes affecting the traditional relationship between religion and state in the Saudi kingdom. First, it has increased role differentiation between the religious and political spheres. Second, it has routinized state control of a broad range of areas that were formerly dominated by religion and the religious establishment. Subsequently to this routinization, the ulama lost many of their traditional functions and became a pressure group limited to exerting influence over the government's activities and policies but never acting as an autonomous center of power. To understand the position and role of the ulama in the newly founded structures, it is necessary to outline the evolution and characteristics of the country's administrative system.

Environmental Factors Affecting the Administrative Transformation of the Polity

The 1932 declaration of Saudi Arabia as a unified kingdom did not in reality affect the traditional administrative structures that had existed in the country. Indeed, the transition from fragmented regional governments to a centralized administrative structure took place only two decades later. Although centralized and modern administrative structures had existed in the Hejaz, other parts of the Saudi domain were administered in the traditional manner. Some administrative structures were created in the 1930s in Hasa and Najd, but they were largely limited in scope and were ad hoc in nature.

As a consequence of the diversity of administrative structures in the country, the extent of role differentiation between the religious and political spheres and the degree of the extension of government jurisdiction over areas that were traditionally controlled by religion and the religious establishment varied from one region to another. In Najd, functional differentiation between the religious and political domains was minimal. This region was hardly subjected to external influences prior to the 1930s and consequently preserved its cultural homogeneity. It was ruled by Ibn Saud through Crown Prince Saud, who acted as an administrative governor and as the personal representative of the king. A number of local umara acted as the king's representatives in their areas. Assisting the umara in day-to-day activities was a corps of ulama, who acted as judges and imams of mosques, as well as some financial administrators and police officers. With the exception of the ulama who were responsible to their superiors in Riyadh, all other administrators were accountable to the amir, who was accountable to the governor, who in turn was accountable to the king.

In contrast to Najd, Hejaz was influenced by foreign administrative systems, especially those of Egypt and Turkey. A number of administrative structures existed prior to the Saudi conquest of the region. For instance, Mecca had several departments such as health, municipal affairs, water supplies, and the judiciary, all coordinated by the City Council under the direct control of the Sherifi ruler. These structures remained intact following the Saudi take-over but fell under the direct control of Faisal, the governor of Hejaz.

The difference in the administrative background between the Hejaz and Najd regions would not be of great significance had it not been for differences in the educational systems of the two regions that subsequently determined, enforced, and perpetuated certain patterns in the newly founded administrative structures. Although Hejaz had a number of secular schools at the turn of the century, it was not until 1938 that secular elementary education was introduced into Najd. Moreover, whereas the ulama were influential in shaping the educational system in Najd and consequently maintained the religious orientation of the curriculum, the Hejazi educational system was more secular in nature and was oriented toward satisfying the needs of a differentiated and complex administration.

The immediate outcome of the differences in the educational system between the two regions was the control by Hejazis of key administrative positions that required secular education. Moreover, whereas Najdis saw in religious education a vehicle for social mobility, many Hejazis attended secular schools and were in a better position to meet the demands of the newly structured institutions.[1] With the centralization of administration in the 1950s, however, and following the increase in the number of Najdis who attained secular education, Najdi representation in the country's administration witnessed a shift in favor of this region.

Oil Economy as a Determinant of Administrative Change

The development of an oil economy affected not only the creation of complex administrative structures but also the overall orientation of the political system. Prior to his death in 1953, Ibn Saud witnessed the drastic increase in his country's wealth—from $200,000 prior to World War I to $10 million in the interwar period; $60 million in 1948; $160 million in 1952; and $250 million in 1953.[2]

The emphasis on oil revenues, as a factor affecting the government services as opposed to the development of new social classes in Saudi Arabia, is dictated by the nature both of the Saudi society and of the oil industry itself. Three factors have minimized the impact of the oil industry:[3] The first is the background of the Saudi society. The oil industry penetrated a society that had no industrial tradition. Legislative and institutional mechanisms were developed in recent years in order to regulate industrial activities to satisfy existing needs and demands. A second factor that minimized the sociopolitical impact of the oil industry is attributed to the nature of the industry. As T. W. Schultz wrote, this industry

[is] not particularly effective in transmitting new knowledge to other sectors or in training workers who acquire skills which serve them well when they enter upon other kinds of work. The techniques of production

in mining and oil tend to be specific and do not lend themselves to useful application in other sectors. Accordingly, as far as the needs of other industries are concerned, few of the techniques of mining and oil are useful to them and few workers are trained in mining and oil from which others can recruit their skilled labor force.[4]

In addition, the oil industry is a one-sided developer given that it does not require a drastic expansion of the transport and power systems. It uses its own facilities and requires little in the way of public services.[5] Finally, the third factor is the remote location of the industry, which limits its impact on the society.

Despite the minimal effects of the industry, the mighty spending power that resulted from oil revenues had shocked the stationary economy of the country.[6] Oil revenues became the most significant single source from which the state's revenues were drawn. In 1932, Saudi government revenues reached 12 million riyals, 60 percent of which came from the hajj. By the year Ibn Saud died, state revenues were 757 million Saudi riyals, 90 percent of which were drawn from oil.[7]

The major problem associated with the tremendous increase in wealth was the fact that until 1959 no distinction existed between the finances of the state and those of the royal family. True to Max Weber's ideal type of patrimonial rule, Ibn Saud and his successor, King Saud, considered the country's wealth to be their own. Even in the first budget ever to be introduced in Saudi Arabia in 1958–1959, the royal household was assigned 17 percent of the budget, to be spent at the discretion of the king; an additional 19 percent was entered under the category of "other expenditures," to be decided by the king as well.

Instead of spending this wealth on development projects, Ibn Saud singled out for special favors and privileges his forty-two sons, his five brothers and their descendants, and the large clans of the Jiluwi, Sudayri, and Al Shaykh, all of whom were related to the royal family. Wahhabi puritanism, which integrated the tribal society and legitimated Ibn Saud's conquests and rule, proved to be incompatible with extreme affluence. As H. St. John Philby describes it,

One by one, at first furtively and later more brazenly, the inhibitions of the old Wahhabi regime went by the board. In the name of military efficiency, the once forbidden charms of music were openly paraded on the palace square. . . . The forbidden cinema reared its ogling screens in scores of princely palaces and wealthy mansions to flaunt the less respectable products of Hollywood before audiences which would have blushed or shuddered at the sight but ten or fifteen years ago.[8]

Whereas Ibn Saud was able to maintain his patrimonial rule through his charismatic personality and the disbursement of financial favors, King Saud failed miserably when he attempted to emulate this pattern of authority. Saud lacked both the charisma and the ability of his father to persuade men and recognize pressing needs. Despite colossal oil revenues, there were few improvements in the living conditions of Saudis; the country's economy became handicapped by serious inflationary pressures. A weak leader with extravagant habits, Saud was unable to arrest the social and moral disintegration of Saudi society, nor was he skillful enough to meet the external socialist challenge posed by Nasser.

In an attempt to avoid increased popular dissatisfaction with Saudi rule, the royal family and ulama leaders transferred the executive functions of Saud to Crown Prince Faisal in 1958. Although Saud recovered these powers in 1960, Faisal continued to be the decision-maker in the polity. It was not until 1964 that Saud was deposed and Faisal was proclaimed king by the royal family and leading ulama.[9]

Under Faisal, the erosion of Saudi political legitimacy was controlled, and the system he bequeathed to King Khalid in 1975 proved to be capable of adapting to change and confronting external political challenges. Faisal reasserted the traditional legitimacy that is the sine qua non of patrimonial rule and developed a complex bureaucratic structure parallel to, but interlocked with and subordinate to, the royal family, so as to enhance the system's capabilities and performance.

The structural changes that occurred in the Saudi political system took place after the discovery of oil in the kingdom, following the realization by Saudi rulers of the need for political change. The resultant change, however, must not be seen as a conscious desire to radically transform the society; rather, it was more in the nature of an adjustive response of patrimonial rule intended to preserve the regime's basic values and characteristics in a changing environment.

Role Differentiation and Institutional Complexity

The presence of differentiated and complex administrative structures enhances the capability of the political system to manipulate its environment. As the political system confronts a wide range of areas that require state intervention, the pressures to develop complex administrative institutions become tremendous. If the political elite desires to maintain its position in society, it must develop these institutions.

Prior to the 1950s, when Ibn Saud realized the need to develop modern administrative institutions, political life in the kingdom revolved around the king, through whom both the executive and legislative powers were exercised. He surrounded himself with advisers who enjoyed his personal trust. The advisers "never demanded, seldom suggested, and only advised when advice was actively sought" by the king.[10]

Following the conquest of Hejaz in 1926 and the subsequent unification of the kingdom in 1932, Ibn Saud needed a more effective administrative structure to meet the ever-increasing economic and social needs generated by oil revenues. While preserving the patrimonial character of his authority, Ibn Saud laid the structural foundation for more differentiated and complex bureaucratic institutions. Although all legislative and executive powers are concentrated in the person of the king, who is the chief-of-state, the prime minister, the commander-in-chief of the armed forces, and the imam of the community, the king's orders, decrees, and policies are channeled downward and implemented by the Council of Ministers.[11]

The present Council of Ministers was preceded by ad hoc committees and administrative institutions. Following the conquest of Mecca in 1924, the Domestic Council of Mecca was created and included in its membership twenty-five deputies representing different interest groups in the city, including the ulama. This council was headed by Ibn Saud's son, Prince Faisal, and its activities included the following: the review of the city's judicial system, the issuance of regulations concerning pilgrimage and *awqaf*, the supervision of religious education, the issuance of commercial laws, and the establishment of a judicial committee to settle disputes according to Islamic and tribal laws.[12] Following the annexation of Jeddah in 1925, the Domestic Council was replaced by the Instructive Committee. This committee, too, was headed by Prince Faisal. It included three members appointed by Ibn Saud and eight elected in a secret ballot by representatives of the major interest groups in the Hejaz, including the ulama. Ibn Saud authorized the committee to assist Prince Faisal in administering the region. Two years later, Ibn Saud established the Committee of Investigation and Reform to review the government's organizational structure.[13] This committee recommended the unification of the country's administrative regions as well as the creation of a national advisory council to represent regional interests. These recommendations were implemented by the establishment of an Advisory Council with eight members appointed by the king, four of whom were appointed after consultation with community leaders, including the ulama. To broaden national representation, the eight members were drawn from the Hejaz and Najd regions. Ibn Saud empowered the Advisory Council to formulate socioeconomic policies, supervise the expenditures of government departments and agencies, and act as a legislative body.[14]

Despite the Advisory Council's formal powers, its decisions were subject to approval by the king. Its jurisdiction and activities were further weakened by two developments: First, a Council of Deputies was created in 1930 to assist Faisal in the administration of the Hejaz region; second, a Council of Ministers was established in 1953 to act as Ibn Saud's cabinet.

The Council of Deputies was established in recognition of the relatively advanced administrative background of the Hejaz. It served as a central agency for coordination of activities among branches of government organizations in the Hejaz region and the Advisory Council as well as other national agencies. As a result of the expansion of government operations throughout the country, the Council of Deputies acquired legislative and executive powers that were derived from the king. Resulting from the creating of the Council of Ministers in 1953 and the subsequent centralization of administration in the country, the Council of Deputies was dismantled and the Council of Ministers became the sole national decisionmaking agency.

The Council of Ministers

The Council of Ministers was created by Ibn Saud in 1953 to act as a central agency for all existing and future departments and agencies. Its membership was made up of existing ministers and was headed by Ibn Saud. The royal decree establishing the council dealt with five areas: (1) organization of the council; (2) jurisdiction of the council; (3) the council's procedures; (4) jurisdiction of the president of the council; and (5) divisions of the council, that is, the council cabinet.[15] Accordingly, the council is headed by the king and, in his absence, by the crown prince; it consists of the king's ministers, advisers, and all those whose attendance at the council is desired by the king; its jurisdiction is outlined in Article 7 of the royal decree, which states that "state policy within the country and abroad shall be under the surveillance of the Council of Ministers."[16] All council decisions "shall not come into effect until they have been sanctioned by His Majesty the King."[17]

The structure and functions of the council were modified by a royal decree on May 12, 1958, which redefined and clarified the council's jurisdictions and created the post of deputy prime minister. The decree stipulated that members of the council are responsible to the prime minister (i.e., the crown prince), who is responsible to the king. Moreover, the prime minister has the right to appeal to the king for the dismissal of any member of the council. The relative weakness of the king's powers as expressed in the 1958 royal order came into existence as a result of the royal family's dismay with King Saud's rule. It was not surprising, therefore, that after Faisal's assumption of power in 1964 the king again assumed the position of prime minister.

The fusion of all powers in the person of the king in 1964 reestablished the supremacy of the monarch and defined the role of the council as the only manager of the country's socioeconomic, administrative, and political affairs. It is the effective arm of the king, and, subject to the king's approval, it has the exclusive jurisdiction to pass laws, initiate policies, and oversee their implementation.

The council's policies and decisions are implemented by a complex bureaucratic structure that has evolved throughout the years from a small number of disjointed departments and ministries to the present system, which exhibits phenomenal centralization. This structure is divided into three components: (1) ministries; (2) independent departments and bureaus; and (3) public agencies.[18]

Until 1951, only three ministries existed—the Ministry of Foreign Affairs (established in 1930), the Ministry of Finance (1932), and the Ministry of Defense (1946). The structure and activities of these ministries was rudimentary. The Ministry of Finance, for example, was administered by Ibn Saud's treasurer, Shaykh Abd Allah al-Sulayman, whose main function was to meet Ibn Saud's personal needs and demands. But its structure and activities today bear no resemblance to those of its predecessor. This ministry has become the most complex and influential of all governmental institutions. It is staffed by highly qualified personnel whose activities and decisions have a direct bearing upon all other departments and ministries.[19]

During the period from 1951 to 1954, the ministries of Interior, Education, Agriculture, Communication, Commerce and Industry, and Health were established. Between 1960 and 1962, the ministries of Petroleum and Mineral Resources; Labour and Social Affairs; Pilgrimage and Awqaf; Information; and Justice were created. Finally, in 1975, six additional ministries, as well as three Ministers of State Without Portfolio, were established, thus bringing the total number to twenty-three. Among the ministries created in 1975 were Public Works and Housing; Industry and Power; Telegraph, Post, and Telephone; Planning; Higher Education; and Municipal and Rural Affairs.

Independent departments and bureaus exist in the state administration. These include the General Personnel Bureau, the Central

Planning Commission, the Grievance Board, the General Department of Intelligence, the Advisory Council, the National Guard, and the Committees for Commanding the Good and Forbidding Evil.[20] These departments and bureaus enjoy relative autonomy, for they report directly to the prime minister (i.e., the king), but general personnel rules and procedures apply to these organizations as if they were ministries.

Finally, to avoid general governmental rules and procedures, which may hinder the activities of certain agencies, the Council of Ministers created public agencies in the 1960s. These include the railroad system, the Institution of Petroleum and Minerals, Saudi Arabian Airlines, the Institute of Public Administration, King Saud University, the Petroleum and Minerals College, the Institution of Social Security, the Centre for Research and Economic Development, Saudi Arabian Monetary Agency, the Agricultural Bank, and the Red Crescent. Though formally attached to a ministry, each agency is governed by an executive board that, in several cases, is headed by a minister and includes the membership of deputy ministers as well as the director general of the agency itself.[21]

The Bureaucratization of the Ulama

The expansion in government administrative structures was accompanied by increased jurisdiction of these structures over a large number of societal areas, including those formerly regulated by religion and the religious establishment. For example, the jurisdiction and activities of the Domestic Council profoundly affected the position of the ulama in two ways: First, although the ulama were represented in the council, their representation was limited to two members, thus minimizing their presence and influence. Second, the council's jurisdiction affected areas that formerly came under the exclusive control of the ulama, such as the administration of *awqaf*, religious schools, and education. The extent of the ulama's participation in the newly founded structures was influenced by the needs and orientation of the political sphere— the ulama were given prominence when religious legitimation was needed, and they assumed a secondary position when their stance contradicted that of the ruler or when other sources of legitimacy were invoked. As the process of territorial shaping neared completion, the ulama lost whatever limited autonomy they had enjoyed; they became paid civil servants whose status, income, and general activities were governed by state regulations and objectives.

The incorporation of the ulama into the state administration routinized the use of religion and the religious establishment as a source of legitimacy. The ulama's role in society and their activities in the administrative structure were channeled through the following fields and agencies: the Committees for Commanding the Good and Forbidding Evil; the Directorate of Religious Research, Ifta', Da'wa, and Guidance; religious education; the Ministry of Justice; preaching and guidance of Islam at home and abroad; supervision of girls' education; supervision of mosques and *awqaf;* notaries public; and finally, spreading Islam and consolidating Saudi international prestige through the activities of Muslim organizations such as the World Muslim League and the World Assembly of Muslim Youth. The following description of the general activities of three of these agencies, as well as of the role of the ulama in the present judicial system, will enable us to assess their role and position in the country's administrative system.

The Committees for Commanding the Good and Forbidding Evil

The need to establish effective structures of political authority became more imperative as the process of territorial expansion advanced. Ibn Saud realized the necessity of developing an administrative system that would meet the peculiar needs of Wahhabism as well as accommodate his political objectives. Consequently, his position vis-à-vis the religious establishment was modified to meet emerging needs. Thus, the Committees for Commanding the Good and Forbidding Evil, initially established to enforce Wahhabi principles, were incorporated into the state machinery. Moreover, whenever Wahhabi principles conflicted with Ibn Saud's political needs, the latter prevailed. The conclusion of agreements with the British, the elimination of the Ikhwan, the introduction of secular education, and the influx of non-Muslims into the kingdom to develop the oil industry are instances in which Ibn Saud's objectives of development prevailed.

The initial impulse for founding the Committees for Commanding the Good and Forbidding Evil is attributed to Shaykh Abd al-Aziz Ibn Abd al-Latif Al Shaykh, who, in 1903, enforced the observance of Wahhabi principles in Riyadh.[22] As the Saudi state expanded throughout Najd and the Hasa, Ibn Saud institutionalized the shaykh's activities by formally establishing committees with similar functions. These committees were headed by Shaykh Abd al-Aziz Al Shaykh and included Shaykh Abd al-Rahman Ibn Ishaq Al Shaykh, Shaykh Omar Ibn Hassan Al Shaykh, and Shaykh Abd al-Latif Al Shaykh. The committees were empowered to arrest, bring to trial, and imprison those found guilty of offending Wahhabi teachings.

A number of posts were opened for the enforcers (*mutawi'a*) in Riyadh and other Saudi cities and towns. A police officer and a director were installed at each post. The director was responsible to the committees' director general, a position usually held by a member of Al Shaykh. All key matters pertinent to the committees were decided by the committees' director general, who in turn received instructions from the king. Despite the existence of an organizational network, the exact duties of enforcers remained undefined, and the promotion and dismissal policies were never specified. It was not until the 1960s that the general regulations governing the Saudi civil service were extended to the committees.

In enforcing Wahhabi principles and establishing control over society, the activities of the *mutawi'a* often covered a wide range of areas. They policed market areas to prevent mingling between men and women and ensured that no individual violated public morality, that merchants and traders did not defraud the consumer, that no places of entertainment were established, that no musical instruments were manufactured or sold, that no paintings depicting humans or animals were made or sold, that men did not wear silk or gold, and that members of the community attended public prayers. They also enforced the prohibitions against smoking and alcohol, and made certain that men followed the *Sunna* in lengthening their beards and shaving off their moustaches.

The restrictions enforced by the *mutawi'a* were in compliance with Wahhabi principles. The application of these principles enabled Ibn Saud to control all the activities of his citizens and to consolidate his rule. It was therefore not surprising that Ibn Saud extended the *mutawi'a* system to the Hejaz region in the late 1920s. The task of forming this network in the Hejaz was delegated by Ibn Saud to Chief Qadi Abd Allah al-Bulayhid, who in turn requested Shaykh Abd Allah al-Shaybi to organize committee posts throughout the region. To justify the extension of the committees to the Hejaz, Abd Allah al-Bulayhid asked Shaykh Muhammad Bahjat al-Bitar, a leading Meccan theologian, to compose writings explaining the principle of commanding the good and forbidding evil and the duties of the *mutawi'a*.[23] Although Shaykh Abd Allah al-Shaybi headed the committees in the Hejaz, ultimate responsibility for the direction and policies of the committees rested with Prince Faisal, governor of the region. In turn, Faisal was accountable to his father, Ibn Saud.

Whereas Ibn Saud was interested in the *mutawi'a* as a mechanism of social control, some *mutawi'a* viewed themselves as guardians of Wahhabi principles and as existing beyond the control of the ruler. In their diligent attempt to enforce Wahhabi principles, the *mutawi'a* opposed some of Ibn Saud's policies. To curb the *mutawi'a*, Ibn Saud issued a royal decree in 1930 incorporating the Committees for

Commanding the Good and Forbidding Evil into the Directorate General of the police force. He stripped the *mutawi'a* of the power of arrest, which they had hitherto enjoyed, and restricted their function to reporting violations to the police. In case of a dispute between the committees' director general and the director general of the police force, the decree provided for the king to act as arbitrator.

The 1930 decree established the modality that defined both the position of the *mutawi'a* within the Saudi administrative structure and the nature of their activities. Although the committees are collectively considered to form an independent bureau and its director general, Shaykh Abd al-Aziz Ibn Abd Allah Ibn Hassan Al Shaykh, was assigned ministerial status in 1976, their role was relegated to a status subservient to that of the state bureaucracy. As the country's administrative structure became more complex in recent decades, the *mutawi'a* were restricted to enforcing public attendance at prayers. The ministries of Commerce, Interior, Health, Finance and National Economy, Agriculture, and Justice, as well as the municipalities, today perform the many duties that were traditionally undertaken by the enforcers. A considerable number of the committee members are now aged and illiterate and lack the basic education expected of religious enforcers. The general decline in the caliber of the *mutawi'a* may be attributed to the lack of specific policies governing recruitment, promotion, and dismissal. *Mutawi'a* recruits are not required to pass entrance exams or possess any academic training. Entrance eligibility is confined to "good religious and social behavior"; promotion is determined by seniority, and dismissal is rare.

The Committees for Commanding the Good and Forbidding Evil were initially created by Ibn Saud to enforce observance of Wahhabi principles and subsequently to control the social behavior of members of the community. The committees' duties covered a wide range of areas of social conduct and provided Ibn Saud with the mechanism to consolidate his authority. As Ibn Saud's authority became well entrenched in the region, and as the process of creating a modern administrative structure succeeded, the *mutawi'a* institution was no longer needed. Instead of eliminating the *mutawi'a*, a measure that might antagonize the ulama, Ibn Saud incorporated this institution into the civil service and stripped it of effective power.

The Directorate of Religious Research,
Ifta', Da'wa, and Guidance

Like the Committees of Commanding the Good and Forbidding Evil, the Directorate of Religious Research, Ifta', Da'wa and Guidance is an independent state department that accounts directly to the king in his capacity as prime minister.[24] It publishes religious books propagating Wahhabi views and principles and distributes them upon request. It also sponsors research projects on Islam and Wahhabism, organizes seminars for training preachers, and sends preachers on foreign assignments. The symbolic consequence of the publication and distribution of religious texts is the projection of Saudi rule as the propagator of Islam, as well as the reaffirmation of its identification with Wahhabism. Among the books published and/or distributed by the directorate, we can note the following:

- a number of books written by or about Shaykh Muhammad Ibn Abd al-Wahhab
- Abd al-Rahman Ibn Muhammad Ibn Qasim al-Asmi al-Hanbali, *Tahrim Halq al-Lihi* (The Religious Prohibition of Shaving Off Beards)
- Shaykh Sulayman Ibn Muhammad al-Hamidi, *al-Turuq al-Shari'ya li hal al-Mashakel al-Zawjiya* (Legal Ways of Solving Marital Problems)
- Shaykh Hamad Ibn Nasser Ibn Uthman Ibn Mu'amar, *Irshad al-Muslimin fi al-Rad ala al-Quburiyin* (The Guidance of Muslims in Answering Those Who Advocate Visitation of Graves)
- Muhammad Sultan al-Masumi al-Maki, *Hal al-Muslim Mulzam bi Itiba' Madhhab Mu'ayan mina al-Madhahib al-Arbi'a?* (Is the Muslim Obliged to Follow a Certain School of the Four Islamic Schools?)
- Abd al-Rahman Ibn Nasser al-Sa'di, *Hukm Shurb al-Dukhan* (The Religious Opinion on Smoking Tobacco)

In addition to its publication and distribution of religious texts, the directorate issues *fatwa*s on questions submitted to it by the king, government agencies, and the public at large. Its activities and members are directed by the king. Royal Decree number 1/137, issued in 1971, specified that members of the Higher Council of the Ifta' are to be appointed by the king. Their function, the decree noted, is "to express opinion based on the shari'ah regarding matters submitted to them by the *wali al-amr*, i.e., the King, to recommend policy on religious matters to guide the *wali al-amr*; and to issue fatwas to guide Muslims in the areas of *aqida, ibadat,* and *mu'amalat.*"[25] The same decree named fifteen leading ulama to the directorate.[26] What is interesting in the directorate's composition is that of the fifteen members only one is from Al Shaykh. The minimal representation of Al Shaykh in this vital religious body is surprising, but it could be viewed as a continuation of Ibn Saud's policy of not allowing any one group to wield more power than the royal family. Indeed, the representation and influence of Al Shaykh in religious activities has declined since the 1940s. Although members of Al Shaykh are presently ministers of Higher

Education, Justice, and Agriculture and Water, the major religious positions of the director general of Religious Research, Ifta', Da'wa, and Guidance, the president of the Muslim League, as well as the more junior positions in religious or religiously inspired institutions are no longer held by Al Shaykh. Moreover, while the traditional career pattern of Al Shaykh has focused on the religious profession, some Al Shaykh members are increasingly receiving secular education and holding secular positions. A survey of thirty-three names of Al Shaykh students registered at Riyadh University in 1979–1980 showed that only thirteen were registered in religious studies, whereas the remaining twenty were pursuing secular studies ranging from business administration to dentistry.[27]

World Assembly of Muslim Youth

Although the activities of the Directorate of Religious Research, Ifta', Da'wa, and Guidance are mostly confined to Saudi Arabia, other agencies have been established by the Saudi government to spread Islam and enhance its prestige among world Muslims. Although Wahhabism is the Saudi point of reference at home, Islamic solidarity is projected as a prime consideration affecting Saudi foreign policy. In a 1979 memorandum submitted by al-Ma'had al-Islami in Riyadh to the Islamic Secretariat for the Celebration of the Fourteenth Hijirah Century, islamic solidarity is defined as

> the mobilization of the intellectual, material and spiritual resources of the ummah in pursuit of commonly and clearly defined socio-economic and cultural goals. Islamic solidarity can be pursued in a framework that involves total acceptance of the requirements which arise from total commitment to Islam; the creation of, and commitment to, new institutions . . . which undertake specialized functions for the ummah as a whole across national, ethnic, linguistic and other boundaries that now divide the Islamic community.[28]

To achieve Islamic solidarity, a number of permanent agencies and organizations were established. An important but little-known government organization whose activities attempt to assert Saudi leadership among Muslim states is the World Assembly of Muslim Youth (WAMY). Headquartered in Riyadh, WAMY was established in December 1972 following a meeting of the representatives of world Muslim youth organizations, which was sponsored by the Saudi Ministry of Education. The objectives of WAMY are

> to serve the ideology of Islam through the propagation of tawhid; to strengthen the sense of pride in Islam among Muslim youth and to arm

them with rational bases and full confidence in the supremacy of the Islamic system over all other systems; and to help them practice Islamic teachings in all their activities; to support Muslim youth and student organizations all over the world and to help them implement their plans and programs whenever possible; to guide and help Muslim youth to set up professional organizations; to take a leading part in the existing professional organizations and to help them perform their Islamic role in building the Islamic nation and to confront the existing challenge.[29]

The Saudi government finances WAMY's activities, which include the building of mosques and religious schools abroad, the sponsoring of preachers' visits to Muslim communities abroad, the hosting of annual conferences for representatives of Muslim youth organizations, and the publication and distribution of religious texts.[30] Consistent with the government's two-pronged policy of affirming the religious character of the state while not allowing the ulama to direct or judge the state's activities, WAMY's policy and activities are planned and administered by secular-educated Saudis. WAMY's secretary general, for example, holds a Ph.D. in international relations from the University of Pennsylvania, and almost all the organization's personnel have a secular education.[31] In addition, a survey of the books published and/ or distributed by WAMY reveals the use of religion to be an instrument of legitimation. Although most of these books are introductory texts on Islam, some deal with specialized subjects such as *jihad*, the Islamic economic order, and the Islamic legal system. The most prominent of these books are the writings of Sayid Qutub, Abul A'la Maududi, Muhammad Qutub, and Abd al-Qadir Awda.[32] They carry a message that is consistent with the Saudi ideological interpretation of Islam: "Islam is the best system to be found on this earth. . . . [It] is the only means to regain honour, leadership and social justice."[33]

The Ulama and the Judicial System

The interpretation of the *shari'ah* principles has traditionally been the ulama's exclusive domain. The importance of this function is dictated by the fact that the *shari'ah* regulates all human activities. As outlined in the *Quran* and the *Sunna*, and elaborated by the ulama through *ijma'* (consensus) and *qiyas* (analogy), the *shari'ah* is a comprehensive code of God's commands and recommendations laid down for human guidance. The principles of the *shari'ah* cover all areas of human activity and conduct:

How and what to eat, when to wash, what to wear, how and when to pray and fast—these and similar matters are treated on the same basis and with just as much meticulous concern as matters more strictly legal, such as marriage and divorce, or commercial transactions, or crime. Governing the whole range of man's relations with God and society, and in the absence of any organized Muslim church hierarchy, the shari'ah is incomparably the central institution of Islam.[34]

When Ibn Saud extended his rule over the Hejaz region, and prior to the unification of the Saudi judicial system in 1927, three distinct systems of law existed. The first was that of the Hejaz, with an Ottoman orientation in which the Hanafi and Shafi'i interpretations were predominant. The second was the system of Najd, whereby each governor, assisted by a *qadi,* solved disputes submitted to him or referred them to the *qadi.*[35] The rigid Hanbali tradition prevailed in this region. The third judicial system was the tribal law, under which conflicting parties referred disputes to the head of the tribe, whose decisions were based on traditions and customs.[36]

Whereas Ibn Saud's initial desire was to maintain Ottoman laws in the Hejaz, the Ikhwan considered these laws antithetical to the *shari'ah* and demanded their abolition. To counter the Ikhwan's demands, Ibn Saud solicited the opinion of his ulama, hoping for a more tolerant and temperate attitude. However, on February 11, 1927, the ulama issued a *fatwa* that supported the Ikhwan's position by noting ". . . and as to the laws, if there be any of them [Ottoman laws] in the Hejaz, it will be immediately abolished and nothing except the pure shari'ah will be applied."[37]

Neither the *fatwa* nor the demands of the Ikhwan were able to influence Ibn Saud's decision to maintain Ottoman secular laws. Indeed, Ibn Saud was in no mood to allow the ulama to control his political objective of initiating change in his realm. Consequently, a royal order sanctioning the existing laws of the Hejaz was issued four months after the proclamation of the *fatwa.* Instructing Prince Faisal, governor of the region, the order noted that "the legal rulings of Ottoman law should remain in effect. We have not repealed them nor have we issued laws replacing them. . . . We accept your suggestion concerning the maintenance of these laws."[38]

In addition to the retention of Ottoman laws in the Hejaz region, the Saudi legal system of the period was not confined to the Hanbali school. As early as August 1927, Ibn Saud instructed his judges in the Hejaz that "as to what school of law [the court] should apply, it is not restricted to any particular school. Rather, the court decides according to what appears to it applicable from any of the schools and there is no difference between one school or another."[39] The same theme was reiterated two years following the unification of the country, when Ibn Saud noted that "we are not bound by one school of law to the exclusion of another. Whenever strong evidence is lacking, we adopt the opinion of Imam Ahmad Ibn Hanbal."[40]

In the early period of the creation of the Saudi state, Ibn Saud maintained the Ottoman laws that prevailed in the Hejaz region and instructed his ulama not to restrict themselves to the Hanbali school. In doing so, Ibn Saud demonstrated his willingness to depart from the rigid Wahhabi interpretation of the *shari'ah* in order to accommodate changing circumstances and needs.

Modification of the Judiciary and
the Loss of Ulama Control

The increase in state jurisdiction and in the complexity of its administrative structures affected all areas of governmental activities, including the judiciary. Although the country's judicial system was simple and lacked differentiation, and although the ulama dominated all judicial activities, the system became highly complex by the 1950s; the ulama's role was confined to the interpretation of the civil and criminal aspects of the *shari'ah* law.

The transformation of the legal system from simple to complex and the ulama's loss of their traditional position in the legal system were attained gradually. The impetus of this change was initiated in 1927 when Ibn Saud issued a decree urging his citizens to bring their complaints to him personally. "Any one who may have a grievance against whoever may be . . . and then hides it, he will be sinning only against himself."[41] The decree noted further that grievances could be relayed to the ruler through a "box of complaints" positioned at the door to the government buildings in Mecca and Riyadh and that the keys to the two boxes are kept by the king himself.[42]

While the box system may have been effective in 1927, changes were needed in 1932. A royal order issued in that year noted that there were four manners through which citizens could express their grievances or bring complaints against individuals or government agencies.[43]

The organizational restructuring of the judicial system took place a year later when a royal decree was issued classifying the court system into three levels: Summary Courts, Shari'ah Courts, and the commission on Judicial Supervision.[44] These courts were confined to Mecca, Jedda, and Medina. Judicial affairs in Najd continued to be administered by a single judge who dealt with all cases.

The jurisdiction of Summary Courts covered cases involving misdemeanors and discretionary and statutory punishments. The Shari'ah Courts had jurisdiction over all cases that are not included in the

jurisdiction of Summary Courts. The Commission on Judicial Supervision consisted of a chairman, a deputy chairman, and three members,
all chosen by the king from among the ulama. In addition to supervising
and inspecting the courts, this commission had the function of judicial
review through the power of confirming or reversing judgments of
the Shari'ah Courts. It also had the power of giving legal opinions
concerning matters not included in the jurisdiction of the Shari'ah
Courts.[45]

This early classification and jurisdictional delimitation of legal
institutions in the Saudi kingdom may be considered the organizational
outline of the present system. Although amendments to the first royal
decree creating the judiciary were made, the structural characteristics
remain the same. For example, while initially Ibn Saud instructed his
ulama not to restrict themselves to the Hanbali interpretation of the
shari'ah, once the unification of the country was accomplished and
Ibn Saud's authority became well entrenched, the ulama were instructed
that legal decisions should be based on the Hanbalite schools "because
of the easy accessibility of its books and its authors' obligation to cite
the legal evidence supporting their views." Concurrently, Ibn Saud
informed his ulama to draw upon the other orthodox schools only in
those cases in which the application of the Hanbalite opinion would
cause strain and incompatibility with public interest. The invocation
of public interest is significant because it gave both the ruler and the
judiciary broad scope in interpreting the *shari'ah.*[46]

The judiciary's adherence to the Hanbalite school was reaffirmed
in a royal decree stating that what was cited in Hanbalite texts should
be applied by the courts. Cases that require legal reasoning and are
not covered in Hanbalite texts should be referred either to the greater
Shari'ah Court or to the Commission on Judicial Supervision.[47] To
routinize the adoption of Hanbali interpretation, six Hanbalite texts
were adopted by the judiciary.[48]

Detailed regulations governing the judiciary were issued in 1938.
These affected the classification of judges. In 1952, a royal decree
elaborated on the classification of judges and increased the complexity
of the court system. The final restructuring of the judicial system
took place in 1962 when Faisal proclaimed his Ten Point Reform
Program, which included, among other things, the creation of a
Ministry of Justice. The implementation of this program took place
in 1970 when the Grand Mufti died. A royal decree was issued creating
a Ministry of Justice and a Supreme Judicial Council.[49] Accordingly,
the Minister of Justice replaced the Grand Mufti.

The Decline of the Role of the Ulama
in the Judiciary

The discovery of oil and the resultant expansion of government services and jurisdiction proved too cumbersome for the Shari'ah Courts to handle. Although Ibn Saud dealt in person with many of the cases involving the interaction with foreigners, by the 1930s he was unable to deal with all situations. The Shari'ah Courts were able to deal with civil and penal matters, but they became helpless in confronting the many conflicts that resulted from the development of an oil economy. Consequently, Ibn Saud delegated judicial authority to committees, commissions, boards, councils, and tribunals, but these were originally of an ad hoc nature and distinct from the judicial system. In recent years, however, many of these structures have acquired a permanent status and now constitute part of the judiciary. Some of these organs, such as the Grievance Board, the Commission on the Settlement of Commercial Disputes, and the Central Committee on Cases of Adulteration, were subsequently incorporated into the judicial system. The personnel responsible for the activities of these organs are secular-educated individuals who have little background in the *shari'ah* law. Their activities dominate the judicial system and have displaced some of the ulama's judicial role.

The Grievance Board, for example, was established in 1955 through a royal decree. The king enjoys tremendous power over the activities of the board. Not only are the chairman and vice-chairman of the board appointed by the king through a royal decree, but the decisions of the chairman are subject to the king's ratification. In cases of a dispute between a minister or head of a department and decisions made by the board, the matter must be referred to the king. In cases where no regulations exist concerning a certain situation, the matter can be settled only by order of the king. Moreover, every six months the chairman of the board must submit to the king a comprehensive report of the board's activity.

The board's jurisdiction includes grievances by citizens against state departments or agencies. It also has the jurisdiction to follow up its investigation of government officials and to adjudicate on disputes pertaining to salaries, retirement, pensions, and decisions of administrative disciplinary councils. In addition, the board receives applications for the execution of foreign judgments and has a representative in tribunals or commissions dealing with bribery offenses, disciplinary actions of military personnel, and violation of the Arab League's policy concerning the boycott of Israel.

The Grievance Board is perhaps the most important of the supplementary organs with judicial functions. This is due in part to its wide jurisdiction and its permanent character. Although not so designated, the board is in fact a tribunal. The central position it occupies in the judicial system is an outcome of the expansion of state jurisdiction and activities and of the inability of the Shari'ah Courts to deal with all issues in so complex a society. The ulama's representation on the board is limited to two *shari'ah* consultants.

In sum, the discovery of oil in the 1930s and the resultant expansion in government activities and jurisdiction necessitated the regulation of these activities through formal rules. It required the creation of institutions to arbitrate the interpretation and application of these rules. The promulgation of laws and the creation of modern administrative and judicial institutions stripped the ulama of their role as the only guardian and interpreter of the most sacred of all Islamic institutions—the *shari'ah*. Instead of enjoying an exclusive monopoly over the interpretation of the *shari'ah*, the ulama now share this role with secular-educated individuals.

As a result of the loss of many of their roles, and resulting from the introduction of laws not present in or derived from the *shari'ah*, the ulama found themselves incapable of exercising their judicial role. A most telling statement expressing the ulama's situation was made in 1967 by the chief judge, who informed members of the Shari'ah Courts that

> we have been informed that some judges have the habit of returning certain cases to the Labour and other offices under the pretext that they fall under the jurisdiction of these authorities. It is recognized that the shari'ah is completely equipped to solve disputes, and to end litigations as well as to clarify every issue. The submission of cases to those authorities implies recognition of the man-made laws and of the regulations repugnant to the provisions of the shari'ah. It also makes the courts appear incapable. . . . You must look into all cases you receive and make your decisions according to the sublime shari'ah. . . . Whenever you have difficulty in doing so, write to us about it.[50]

Conclusion

The development of an oil economy in Saudi Arabia has ushered in a period of increased government activities that necessitated the expansion of state jurisdiction over areas formerly dominated by the religious establishment. It led to the creation of a complex administrative structure to implement these policies. In turn, the expansion of jurisdiction and the corresponding increase in role differentiation between the religious and political spheres resulted in the bureaucratization of the ulama. Indeed, the ulama in the current Saudi state are dependent on the state for their survival. They are paid civil servants whose activities are determined by the needs of the political sphere. Ulama leaders are appointed by the king, and ulama activities are regulated by state laws.

Following the introduction of secular laws to regulate the many state activities, the role of the ulama became confined to the interpretation of the civil and criminal aspects of the *shari'ah*, whereas commercial, labor, and international laws, to name only three, are formulated and interpreted by secular-educated individuals. The state took over religion for the purpose of restructuration to bring its beliefs and institutions into conformity with national objectives. The activities of WAMY and the Directorate of Research, Ifta', Da'wa, and Guidance are geared toward the presentation of Wahhabi principles that coincide with state objectives, and toward projecting the Saudi rulers as the protectors and propagators of Islam. In effect, the political sphere enhanced its legitimacy through the rationalization of policies in religious terms. The emergence and increased role of secular-educated individuals in the system reflects the overall position of the political sphere in relation to the ulama: While religion remains an important source of legitimation, the ulama's traditional role in evaluating government policy and activities has been reduced.

5
Changing Patterns in the Composition and Orientation of the Political Elite

The study of the composition and orientation of the Saudi political elite provides a basis for assessing the extent to which the role and position of the ulama have changed in the political system. The political elite refers to "those who are most powerful, . . . who direct and control the political system and who are its model of political activity. . . ."[1] Until the 1950s, the Saudi political elite consisted of the royal family, the tribal leaders, and the ulama. The expansion of government services and the complexity of administrative institutions in recent decades have affected the composition and orientation of the country's political elite. First, although the royal family continues to maintain its dominant position, the educational background and career pattern of its members have been altered to accommodate emergent needs. Second, the settlement of bedouins, the invocation of Wahhabism as the state ideology, and the creation of national identity have weakened the role of tribal leaders. Third, as a result of the expansion of jurisdiction and the complexity of institutions, the ulama have lost many of their traditional powers, some of which were incorporated in the newly emergent structures. Fourth, the creation of modern institutions necessitated the recruitment of secular-educated administrators whose educational background and skills bear little resemblance to those of the ulama.

For the most part, the higher civil service positions are held by secular-educated Saudis. Whereas in the past Saudi education was largely religious and controlled by the ulama, by the 1950s the number of secular schools had increased and their graduates had begun to assume key governmental positions. The first Saudi university was the Shari'ah Islamic Law College of Mecca, which opened in 1949. Its curriculum included the traditional subjects of *Quran, hadith,* Arabic language, Arabic history, and Arabic literature. Subsequently, *shari'ah* and Arabic language colleges were opened in Riyadh in 1953 and 1954, respectively, to train judges and teachers. Secular higher education was introduced only in 1957 with the opening of King Saud University in Riyadh. In subsequent years, the College of Petroleum and Minerals, King Abd al-Aziz University, and Imam Saud Islamic University were also established.[2]

The increase in the number of secular-educated administrators was reflected in the increase in the number of ministerial positions they held. Virtually all of the major ministerial portfolios in the 1950s were held by members of the royal family. During this period only one of the nine ministerial positions, that of the minister of commerce, was held by someone other than a prince or his dependent.[3] Between 1954 and 1958 the minister of commerce was a secular-educated member of a prominent Jeddah family. Six of the ministers in this period were princes, and the remaining two, those of health and finance, were former personal advisers to the king. The minister of health after 1954 was the Syrian-born Dr. Rashad Far'oun, who had been King Ibn Saud's personal physician until the latter's death in 1953. The minister of finance was Ibn Saud's personal treasurer, Abd Allah Sulayman; his successor was another personal confidant of the king, Muhammad Surur Saban.[4] The predominance in the 1950s of princes and of the king's confidants in ministerial roles reflects the patrimonial character of the regime. Ministers and administrators were selected primarily on the basis of their proximity to the king rather than for their abilities and achievements.

By the 1960s, appointments of secular-educated commoners to cabinet positions had increased in number. In 1960, King Saud assigned five ministerial posts, two of which had always been held by princes, to nonroyal family members. Four of these new ministers were graduates from Cairo University in their early forties, and the fifth was a thirty-five-year-old graduate of the University of Texas who took over the Ministry of Petroleum and Mineral Resources. To attain their positions, the four combined family background with the newly important asset of secular education. The fifth, Abd Allah al-Tariki, minister of petroleum, was a Najdi who had previously demonstrated his abilities as director of the petroleum department of the Ministry of Finance.[5]

Until 1975, members of the royal family retained five of the fourteen ministerial posts. These five—Interior, Defense, National Guard, Finance, and Foreign Affairs—are the controlling agencies of the national government; with this control, the princes maintained their hold over the political system. Following the 1975 King Khalid cabinet, four of the five ministries continued to be held by family members, whereas the Ministry of Finance was assigned to a secular-educated Najdi, Aba al-Khail. Moreover, the ministries of Municipal and Rural Affairs and of Public Works and Housing were created and assigned to members of the royal family.

The royal family continues to control key administrative positions. In recent years, family members have begun to administer the more junior posts, which require secular education, thereby ensuring the continuity of the regime's patrimonial character.

The Royal Family

The exact size of the royal family is unknown. Some estimates place its number between 3,000 and 5,000 males, while others suggest that there are "hundreds of relatives—brothers and sons, uncles, nephews, cousins, and their wives and children—offspring of each of the . . . Saudi kings."[6] What is known with some certainty, however, is that the large size of the family can be attributed to Ibn Saud's numerous marriages—his means of consolidating his rule through forming alliances with the leading tribes. Ibn Saud, as David Howarth has noted, had "more than three hundred wives, and most of these marriages were motivated by political considerations."[7] After the defeat of Ibn Rashid, for example, Ibn Saud "took all the remaining members of the family of Rashid as his guests to Riyadh, where they lived out their lives at his expense, in reasonable freedom, within his crowded court. . . . He married the principal widow of his murdered rival and accepted the orphan children as his own."[8] One after another, Ibn Saud married into all of the leading tribes and families. As indicated in Table 5.1, he had wives from the Sudayr tribe, the Mutair, the Anaza, and the Dawasir—to name only four.[9]

To appreciate the importance of marriage as an instrument of alliance formation, we must outline the role of kinship as a determinant of social status and role in Saudi Arabia. It is the family, not the individual, that forms the basic social unit. The individual male is responsible for the well-being of his family; he behaves according to his family's status and values; and his social status is dictated largely by that of his family.[10] Although the tribal character of the Saudi society has been radically altered in recent decades as a result of the development of an oil economy and the settlement of bedouins, the family remains the focus of loyalty.[11] In whatever familial group—*a'ilah* (family), *hamulah* (subtribe), *ashirah* (a larger subtribe), or *qabilah* (tribe)—the status and interests of the individual are determined by and subordinated to those of the family.

The political significance of family ties in the case of Saudi Arabia is that family members support one another in their quest for power

TABLE 5.1
The Royal Family: Tribal Affiliations*

Names	Tribal Affiliations
Turki and Saud	Children of Wadha, daughter of Muhammad al-Urayr, Shaykh of Bani Khalid tribe
Faisal	Son of Tarfa, daughter of Shaykh Abd Allah Al Shaykh
Muhammad and Khalid	Children of Mukosara, daughter of Musa'id Ibn Jiluwi Al Saud
Fahd, Sultan, Abd Al Rahman, Turki, Nasir, Salman, and Ahmad	Known as the "Sudayri Seven"; constitute the most influential faction within the Royal Family. Children of Hessa, daughter of Ahmad al-Sudayri
Mansour, Mush'il, and Mut'ib	No information
Sa'd II, Musa'id, and Abd Al-Muhsin	Children of Jawhara, daughter of Sa'd al-Sudayri
Abd Allah	Son of al-Fahda, daughter of 'Asi Ibn Sharim, Shaykh of the Shammar Tribe
Bandar and Fawaz	No information
Talal and Nawaf	Children of Haya, daughter of Sa'd al-Sudayri (Sister of Jawhara)
Thamer, Mamdouh, and Mash'hour	Children of Nauf, granddaughter of Nouri al-Sha'lan, Shaykh of al-Roula tribe

*Information on the Royal Family was gathered through interviews during field research in 1979 and 1980.

and authority. Prince Abd Allah's position in the Saudi power structure, for example, is enhanced by his affiliation with the Shammar tribe, one of the most powerful in the country. Members of this tribe owe allegiance to Abd Allah, who acts as an intermediary between them, the royal family, the king, and the bureaucracy. The position of King Fahd and his six full brothers, collectively known as the "Sudayri Seven," is considered the strongest among members of the royal family not only because of this group's affiliation with the Sudayr tribe through their mother, but also because they are full brothers who control key governmental positions.

Members of the royal family play a vital role in the Saudi political process. Not all family members, however, are engaged in state administration, and not all of them enjoy the same status. The status of the individual within the family and his role in government are determined by two considerations: first, the individual's proximity to the king's immediate family; and second, the individual's generation. Since the death of Ibn Saud in 1953, kingship passed first to his son Saud and, as of 1964, from brother to brother. Saud was the oldest, followed by Faisal. As indicated in Table 5.2, Prince Muhammad should have succeeded Faisal, but he renounced his claim in favor of his younger brother Khalid. Muhammad's renunciation of his claim was forced upon him by the senior members of the family and the ulama because of his personal conduct, which seemed antithetical to Wahhabi puritanism. His disqualification may illustrate the role of the leading ulama in the patrimonial political system—selective involvement and participation. It also demonstrated the powerful role of the senior members of the family in determining succession.

Equal to Muhammad in status are Ibn Saud's living brothers. As indicated in Table 5.3, still living are three of Ibn Saud's brothers, two of whom had aided his drive to expand and consolidate Saudi rule. Because of their age and proximity to Ibn Saud, the three brothers constitute a distinct group whose opinion is highly valued.

The status and role of individuals within the royal family are also influenced by sibling group formations. One of the most influential of these groups is the Sudayri Seven. In addition to the seven brothers, as indicated in Table 5.4, nine members of the Sudayri clan are currently governors of various administrative units in the kingdom, and one was a deputy chairman of the Administrative Council of Medina.

A second collateral branch in the royal family is the Jiluwi group, composed of descendants of a brother of Ibn Saud's grandfather. A member of this group, Abd Allah Ibn Jiluwi, was one of the forty men who, with Ibn Saud, recaptured Riyadh in 1902 and was sub-

TABLE 5.2
The Children of Ibn Saud

Name	Date of Birth	Education	Position
Turki	1900; died in 1919	Court education: religion, politics, and chivalry	No position.
Saud	1902, in Riyadh; died in exile in 1969	Court education	Governor of Najd; Crown Prince; King (1953-1964); was removed by members of the royal family and the ulama for his religious and moral laxity.
Faisal	1906; was assassinated by his nephew in 1975	Court education	Governor of Hejaz, Foreign Minister; Crown Prince; President, Council of Ministers; President, Consultative Council; Chairman of Supreme Planning Board; King (1964-1975).
Muhammad	1912	Court education	Governor of Medina, but did not assume position. Medina was governed on his behalf.
Khalid	1913; died in 1982	Court education	First Deputy Prime Minister; Crown Prince; King (1975-1982), and Prime Minister.
Nasir	1919	Court education	Governor of Riyadh.
Sa'd	1919	Court education	No information.
Fahd	1920	Court education	Minister of Education; Chairman, Administrative Committee in Council of Ministers; Head of Saudi Delegation to the Arab League; Second Deputy Prime Minister; First Deputy Prime Minister; Minister of Interior; Crown Prince; King (1982).
Mansour	1920; died in Paris, 1950	Court education	Chief of Royal Cabinet; Minister of Defense.
Abd Allah	1921	Court education	Commander of National Guard; Second Deputy Prime Minister; Crown Prince.
Bandar	1922	Court education	Director General of Ministry of Interior; prominent businessman.

Name	Year	Education	Description
Sultan	1922	Court education	Member of the Supreme Council of Education, Council of Ministers; Head of Royal Guard; Minister of Agriculture; Minister of Defense and Aviation.
Mash'al	1925	Court education	Succeeded Mansour as Minister of Defense; Minister of Agriculture; Governor of Mecca; retired.
Musa'id	1926	Court education	Major Businessman; no official position.
Abd al-Muhsin	1927	Court education	Minister of Interior; resigned in support of the "Liberal Princes"; Governor of Medina.
Mushari	1930	Court education	Major businessman; no official position.
Mut'ib	1931	Court education	Deputy Minister of Defense; Governor of Mecca.
Talal	1931	Court education	Minister of Transport; Saudi Ambassador to France; Minister of Finance; led the "Liberal Princes" in favor of democratization of regime; leading businessman.
Abd al-Rahman	1931	High School from Saudi Arabia; Military Cadet in California; Diploma of Military Academy, California; B.A. in economics and business administration, Berkeley.	No official position. Leading businessman: founder of the National Gypsum Co.; owner and operator of "model farms" in various provinces; founder and owner of Al Khat Publishing House in Jeddah; founder and owner of Publication and Translation Co. in Damman; co-founder and major shareholder in the Riyadh and Jeddah Electric Power Companies; co-founder and major shareholder in the Eastern Province Electric Co.; owner of a number of cement plants in the country.
Turki II	1932	Court education	Deputy Minister of Defense.
Badr	1932	Court education	Deputy Commander of National Guard; Minister of Communications.
Nawaf	1933	Studied in the U.S., but did not obtain degree.	Chief of Royal Cabinet; succeeded Talal as Minister of Finance; adviser to King Faisal.

Table 5.2 cont.

Nayef	1933	Court education	Governor of Riyadh; Governor of Medina; Deputy Minister of Interior; Minister of State for Internal Affairs.
Fawaz	1934	Court education	Governor of Riyadh; Deputy Governor of Mecca; Governor of Mecca.
Majid	1936	Court education	Minister of Municipal and Rural Affairs.
Salman	1936	Court education	Governor of Riyadh.
Abd al-Ilah	1938	No information	No information.
Ahmad	1939	Court education	Deputy Governor of Mecca.
Satam	1940	Court education	Deputy Governor of Riyadh.
Thamer	1940	No information	No position. Committed suicide in the U.S.
Mamdouh	1941	No information	Leading businessman.
Mash'hour	1941	Court education	Leading businessman.
Hathloul	1941	No information	Leading businessman.
Hamoud	1942	No information	Leading businessman.
Abd al-Majid	1942	No information	Leading businessman.
Muqrin	1942	Air Force Academy, Saudi Arabia, U.S.	Air Force Commander.

TABLE 5.3
The Brothers of Ibn Saud

Name	Education	Position
Faisal Ibn Abd Al-Rahman	Court	Died in 1890. No position held.
Muhammad Ibn Abd Al-Rahman	Court	Died in Riyadh in 1943. No position held.
Saud Ibn Abd Al-Rahman	Court	Died in 1965. Major businessman.
Abd Allah Ibn Abd Al-Rahman	Court	Elder of the Royal Family.
Sa'd Ibn Abd Al-Rahman	Court	Killed in battle in 1915. Commander in Ibn Saud's army.
Ahman Ibn Abd Al-Rahman	No information.	No information.
Musa'id Ibn Abd Al-Rahman	Court	Minister of Finance; Member of Council of Ministers; Chairman of Financial Committee, Council of Ministers; Chairman of Board of Directors, Public Administration Institute; Deputy Chairman of Supreme Planning Board; Chairman of Grievance Board, Ministry of Justice; Minister of Justice.
Abd Al Muhssen Ibn Abd Al-Rahman	Court	No information.

TABLE 5.4
The Sudayri Branch

Name	Position
Turki Ibn Ahmad Ibn Muhammad Al Sudayri	Governor of Jaizan
Musa'id Ibn Ahmad Ibn Muhammad Al Sudayri	Governor of Tabuk
Abd Al Aziz Ibn Abd Allah Ibn Nasir Al Sudayri	Secretary to the Governor of Tabuk
Kahlid Ibn Ahmad Ibn Muhammad Al Sudayri	No information
Muhammad Ibn Ahmad Ibn Muhammad Al Sudayri	No information
Bandar Ibn Ahmad Ibn Muhammad Al Sudayri	No information
Abd Al Rahman Ibn Ahmad Ibn Muhammad Al Sudayri	Governor of Jauf and Sakaka Districts
Abd Al Rahman Ibn Musa''id Ibn Ahmad Ibn Muhammad Al Sudayri	Deputy Chairman of the Administrative Council of Medina
Sulayman Ibn Ahmad Ibn Muhammad Al Sudayri	No information
Abd Allah Ibn Abd Al Aziz Ibn Ahmad Ibn Muhammad Al Sudayri	Inspector, Northwest Frontier, and Governor of Qaryat al-Milh

Nayf Ibn Abd Al Aziz Ibn Ahmad Ibn Muhammad Al Sudayri	Governor of Amlaj
Musa'id Ibn Khalid Ibn Ahmad Ibn Muhammad Al Sudayri	No information
Abd Allah Ibn Sa'd Ibn Abd Al Muhsin Al Sudayri	No information
Nasir Ibn Sa'd Ibn Abd Al Muhsin Al Sudayri	Governor of Al Ghat
Ahmad Ibn Abd Al Muhsin Ibn Sa'd Al Sudayri	Governor of al-'Ula
Abd Al Rahman Ibn Ahmad Ibn Abd Al Rahman Al Sudayri	Governor of Jeddah
Sa'ud Ibn Abd Al Rahman Ibn Turki Al Sudayri	Governor of Baljarshi
Ahmad Ibn Turki Ibn Muhammad Al Sudayri	No information
Nasir Ibn Abd Allah Ibn Nasir Al Sudayri	Governor of al-Wajh

sequently appointed governor of the oil-rich Eastern Province. Following his death in 1941, his son, Saud Ibn Abd Allah, succeeded him in the governorship; following Saud's death, his other son, Abd al-Muhsin, assumed the position. In addition to their control of the Eastern Province, the Jiluwis occupy positions as governors of minor regions. Their importance is reinforced by the fact that the mother of King Khalid and Prince Muhammad as well as the mother of two of King Faisal's sons are from the Jiluwi clan.

The third collateral branch, the Thunayan, are descendants of Thunayan, an older brother of the founder of the Saudi dynasty, Muhammad Ibn Saud. This branch had one Saudi ruler, Abd Allah al-Thunayan (1841–1843), whose descendants moved to Constantinople following the dissolution of the second Saudi state. Although the Thunayans are small in number compared to the other two branches, their importance is derived from the facts that King Faisal's wife, Queen Iffat, is a Thunayan and that her children hold key positions in the state administration as well.

Cutting across the collateral branches are the grandchildren of Ibn Saud. Whether they be Sudayris, Jiluwis, or Thunayans, their views do not as yet carry the same weight as those of their elders. Collectively, however, they represent a distinct group of members of the royal family whose educational background, career pattern, and social outlook differ from those of their elders. This difference reflects the extent to which the polity has changed over the past three decades.

The Royal Family as a Microcosm of Change

The large size of the royal family has enabled it to play the role of the single ruling party that exists in many Arab states, with ascriptive ties and mutual interests acting as the structural and ideological bond among the family members. As we have seen in Table 5.1, members of the family integrate the country's leading tribes through a network of marriage. Tables 5.2 and 5.4 indicate the administrative positions they held and thus the means by which Al Saud was able both to integrate the country's remote regions into the central administration and to administer the positions that ensure the family's control of society.

The ability of the Saud family to maintain control of society is also attributed to its willingness to adapt to and satisfy emergent needs. Referring back to Table 5.2, we find that thirty-two of Ibn Saud's thirty-six children held positions with a direct bearing upon state security. With the exception of Abd al-Rahman, Nawaf, and Muqrin, all had had a court education that emphasized religious instruction. Indicated in Table 5.5, however, is the drastic change over the past three decades in the educational and career patterns of members of the royal family. A number of Ibn Saud's grandchildren and nephews acquired secular education and assumed positions that required secular knowledge. It is erroneous to assume that educational background alone is the determinant of social and political outlook, as the case of Prince Talal demonstrates: Although he received a court education, he subsequently headed the "Liberal Princes" faction, advocated the abolition of the monarchy, and sought refuge in socialist Egypt in 1964. Most important is the royal family's ability to satisfy the needs of the newly created bureaucratic structures from within its ranks; it is through this means that it maintained its control of society.

The success of the royal family in maintaining its position through the acquisition of secular education, and the resultant decrease in the importance of religious education, is best illustrated by the case of the late King Faisal's children. As indicated in Table 5.6, of Faisal's eight male children seven did their secondary education at either the Hun School or the Lawrenceville School in New Jersey. Following graduation, they continued their higher education in the United States and England.[12] The first of Faisal's children to study abroad was Prince Muhammad, who attended both the Hun School and the Lawrenceville School. He earned a degree in business administration in the United States, worked first at the Saudi Arabian Monetary Agency and then as governor of the Saline Water Conversion State Corporation, and finally went into private business.

Another of Faisal's sons, Prince Khalid, now governor of Asir, graduated from the Hun School, studied at Princeton, and transferred to Oxford where he obtained a B.A. degree. Sa'ud Al-Faisal, currently minister of external affairs, studied at Hun and Princeton. Following graduation in 1965 with a B.A. degree in economics, he served for ten years as a deputy to Shaykh Ahmad Zaki al-Yamani in the General Petroleum and Minerals Organization and in the Ministry of Petroleum and Mineral Resources.

Military careers are also pursued by royal family members. Now an officer, Prince Abd al-Rahman graduated from the Hun School and the Royal Military Academy at Sandhurst. Prince Bandar attended Whittier College in California, obtained a B.A. in the United States, and completed a Royal Air Force Pilot training program in Cranwell, England.

The sixth of Faisal's children, Prince Sa'd, received a law degree from Cambridge, was appointed division director in Petromin, and is currently a prominent businessman. Finally, there is Prince Turki, who attended the Hun School, studied at Princeton, and in 1972

TABLE 5.5
The Grandchildren and Nephews of Ibn Saud

Name	Position	Education
Abd al-Rahman Ibn Saud	Director General, Ministry of Finance	B.A. (U.S.)
Bandar Ibn Fahd	Director General, Ministry of Commerce	B.A. (U.S.)
Khalid Ibn Fahd	Deputy Minister of Education	B.A. (U.S.)
Faisal Ibn Abd al-Aziz	Director General of Scholarship and External Relations, Ministry of Education	No information
Muhammad Abd Allah Al Faisal	Director General, Ministry of Education	B.A. (U.S.)
Saud al-Faisal	Deputy Minister of Petroleum and Mineral Resources; Secretary General of Higher Petroleum Council; Minister of Foreign Affairs	B.A. (U.S.)
Fahd Ibn Sultan	Director General of Social Welfare, Ministry of Labor	B.A. (Egypt)
Faisal Ibn Fahd	Director General of Youth Affairs; Chairman of Saudi Olympics Committee	No information
Muhammad Al Faisal	Head of Water Supply Directorate; Deputy Director in Ministry of Agriculture	B.A. (U.S.)

Name	Position	Education
Khalid Al Faisal	Governor of Asir	B.A. (Britain)
Sa'd Ibn Fahd Ibn Abd Al Rahman	Governor of Ha'il	No information
Fahd Ibn Muhammad Ibn Abd al-Rahman	Governor of Qassim	No information
Abd al-Muhsin Ibn Jiluwi	Governor of the Eastern Province	No information
Muhammad Ibn Fahd Jiluwi	Governor of al-Ahsa	No information
Abd Allah Ibn Musa'id Jiluwi	Governor of Northern Territories	No information
Abd al-Aziz al-Thunayan	Major of Riyadh	B.A. (U.S.)
Musa'id Ibn Abd al-Rahman	Minister of Finance; Director of Grievance Board	No information
Khalid Ibn Sultan	Army officer	Military Academy, (Saudi Arabia, U.S.)
Badr Ibn Abd al-Muhsin Ibn Saud	President of the Saudi Arab Arts Society	B.A. (U.S.)
Bandar Ibn Khalid	No official position. Leading businessman: owner and chairman of al-Bandar International Corporation Ltd., for Construction and Real Estate. In 1975, al-Bandar was engaged in constructing 3,000 residential units in Jizan.	Court education
Saud Ibn Abd al-Muhsin	Deputy Governor of Mecca; Director of Health, Housing, and Environment Departments, Central Planning Organization; Director of Coordination, Ministry of Health.	B.A. (Business Administration) (U.S.)

TABLE 5.6
The Children of King Faisal

Name	Education	Position
Abd Allah Ibn Faisal	Court education	Assisted his father in administering Hejaz; Minister of Interior; Minister of Health; leading businessman
Muhammad Ibn Faisal	B.A. (United States)	Head of Water Supply Directorate; Deputy Director of Ministry of Agriculture
Saud Al Faisal	B.A. (United States)	Deputy Minister of Petroleum and Minerals; Secretary General of Higher Petroleum Council; Minister of Foreign Affairs
Sa'd Ibn Faisal	B.A. (Britain)	Prominent businessman
Khalid Ibn Faisal	B.A. (Britain)	Director General of Youth Affairs and Sports; Governor of Asir
Turki Ibn Faisal	B.A. (Britain)	Legal Adviser
Abd al-Rahman Ibn Faisal	Military Academy (Britain)	Army officer
Bandar Ibn Faisal	B.A. (United States) Royal Air Force (Britain)	Air Force officer

graduated from Cambridge, where he took a degree in Shari'ah Law. He now serves as a legal adviser in the present cabinet.

The change in the educational backgrounds and career patterns of members of the royal family indicates its concern with maintaining its position in society as well as its willingness to adapt to changing circumstances. Equipped with survival instinct, the royal family did not resist change; rather, it has controlled and guided its direction. Because of its large size, it relied on its members to assume leadership positions in the newly created institutions. In addition to maintaining monopoly over the key posts, including the first and second deputy premierships as well as the ministries of Defense, National Guard, and Foreign Affairs, members of the family are increasingly assuming control of more junior positions. Whereas in the early period of Saudi rule Ibn Saud's sons served as governors and ministers, members of the present family are in control even of secondary positions in state administration. Muhammad Ibn Abd Allah, for example, is a deputy director in the Ministry of Agriculture; Abd al-Rahman Ibn Saud, Bandar Ibn Fahd, and Fahd Ibn Sultan, to name only three, are either directors or deputy directors of state agencies.

Secular Bureaucrats

The creation of modern administrative institutions has necessitated the recruitment of secular-educated administrators whose educational background and skills are not satisfied by or found among the ulama. Whereas in the 1930s religious education was the necessary requisite for recruitment into the state administration in Najd, by the 1950s it was displaced by secular education. The secularization of the educational system to meet the needs of the newly created administrative institutions and the increase in the number of secular-educated administrators have continued well into the present. Of forty-four high-level officials surveyed in 1972, 65 percent had a secular education. As indicated in Table 5.7, four ministers had traditional education whereas six were secular educated.

The number and influence of secular-educated administrators is even greater at the relatively more junior positions. Only three deputy ministers in the 1972 cabinet, including two members of the royal family, received traditional education; the remaining eleven are secular educated, and eight of these studied at American universities. Moreover, with the exception of the heads of the National Guard and religious organizations, all of the directors of the country's major agencies and corporations are secular educated. The directors of Petromin and the Central Planning Organization in 1972 were two

TABLE 5.7
The Educational Backgrounds of High-Level
Saudi Officials (1972)[13]

Ministries	Minister	Deputy Ministers
Interior	Al Saud	Al Saud
Defense	Al Saud	Al Saud
Finance	Al Saud	B.A. (Cairo)
Pilgrimage	Al Saud	B.A. (Cairo)
Foreign Affairs	Traditional	B.A. (U.S.)
Education	Traditional	B.A. (U.S.)
Communications	Traditional	B.A. (U.S.)
Justice	Traditional	Traditional
Commerce	B.A. (Cairo)	M.A. (U.S.)
Health	B.A. (Cairo)	DDS (Cairo)
Labor	B.A. (Cairo)	M.A. (U.S.)
Information	B.A. (Cairo)	B.A. (U.S.)
Petroleum	M.A. (U.S.)	B.A. (U.S.)
Agriculture	M.A. (U.S.)	M.A. (U.S.)

Saudis who received a Ph.D. and an M.A., respectively, from the United States.

Of the twenty-three ministers in King Khalid's cabinet, excluding members of the royal family, only three received a religious education. As indicated in Table 5.8, the ministers of Justice, of Pilgrimage Affairs and Awqaf, and of Higher Education were educated in religious institutions, while the remaining cabinet members received higher education in the United States, Britain, Egypt, or Lebanon.

The increase in the number of secular-educated ministers should not be viewed as precipitating a dramatic shift in the political system's basic values or orientation. On the contrary, the patrimonial character of the political system persists. The king remains the center of power and loyalties, ministers act more as advisers than as initiators of policy, and ascriptive considerations remain important in determining recruitment to the political system. Moreover, the use of religion and religious symbols to enhance the regime's legitimacy remains a vital and important frame of reference even among the secular-educated ministers and their deputies.

The ministers of Commerce, Industry and Electricity, Planning, and Petroleum and Mineral Resources rationalize many of their policies in religious terms. Minister of Planning Hisham Nazir, for example, is the least exposed of all ministers to religious education and to the influence of the ulama in the affairs of his ministry. He nevertheless

TABLE 5.8
King Khalid's Cabinet: Regional and Educational Backgrounds[14]

---

(1) Dr. Abd al-Rahman Ibn Abd al-Aziz Al Shaykh, Minister of Agriculture; Ph.D. (U.S.)

---

(2) Dr. Sulaiman Abd al-Aziz al-Sulaim, Minister of Commerce:

Was born in 1938. Received his primary and secondary education in Basra, Iraq. Received a B.A. in political science from Cairo University in 1962, an M.A. in international relations in 1966 from the University of Southern California, and a Ph.D. in law from Johns Hopkins University in 1970.

Joined the Ministry of Labor and Social Affairs as director of foreign relations in 1962. In 1963, he became member of the Saudi Delegation to the United Nations conference on "The Application of Science and Technology for the Benefit of the Less Developed Countries." In 1968, was appointed delegate to the United Nations Conference of Ministers of Social Affairs. Appointed minister of commerce by King Khalid in the 1975 cabinet.

In his Ph.D. dissertation, "Constitutional and Judicial Organization in the Kingdom of Saudi Arabia," al-Sulaim noted that the shari'ah is compatible with the modern world. The problem, however, is the existence of "a communication gap between the ulama on the one hand and the technocrats and intellectuals on the other. The latter seem to be unaware of the contribution of the ulama to the stability and continuity in a traditional society; nor are they always appreciative of the wealth of Islamic jurisprudence. The ulama, on their part, have not found the right mode of conveying these qualities to the intellectuals." Sulaiman Abd al-Aziz al-Sulaim, Constitutional and Judicial Organization in the Kingdom of Saudi Arabia (Ph.D. dissertation, Johns Hopkins University), 1970, p. 169.

---

(3) Dr. Abd al-Aziz Abd Allah al-Khuwaiter, Minister of Education:

Was born in Najd in 1927. Received his elementary and secondary education in Saudi Arabia, and a Ph.D. in history from Britain.

In 1965, he headed the Directorate of Supervision and Follow Up; a year later he was appointed vice-rector of Riyadh University by the minister of education. In 1967, al-Khuwaiter joined Faisal's cabinet as minister of health, and in 1975 he became minister of education.

---

(4) Muhammad Aba al-Khail, Minister of Finance and National Economy:

Was born in Najd; Received a B. Com. in 1956 from Cairo University.

Between 1956 and 1962 he served as assistant director in the Bureau of the Minister of Communications, then as director of the same bureau. In 1962, Faisal delegated him to establish an Institute of Public Administration in Riyadh. He headed this institute between 1962 and 1965. In 1970 he became deputy minister of state for Finance and National Economy, and in 1975 he joined King Khalid's cabinet.

---

(5) Dr. Hussein Abd al-Qadir al-Jaza'iri, Minister of Health; M.D. (U.S.)

(Table 5.8 continues)

(6) Hassan Abd Allah Al Shaykh, Minister of Higher Education:

Was born in Mecca in 1933. Tutored by his father Shaykh Abd Allah and received secondary education in Mecca. Obtained a B.A. in Arabic language and Islamic studies from the Mecca Shari'ah College.

He was appointed by his father as a member of the Judiciary Presidium in the Hejaz region (1956-1958). After his father's death in 1958, he became president of the Presidium. In 1962, Crown Prince Faisal appointed him minister of education; in 1975 he joined King Khalid's cabinet as minister of higher education. In addition to his ministerial position, Al Shaykh was appointed by King Faisal to head the Supreme Council of King Abd al-Aziz Research Centre (Darat al-Malik Abd al-Aziz).

---

(7) Dr. Ghazi al-Qusaibi, Minister of Industry and Electricity:

Was born in 1940 in the Hasa region. Received his elementary and secondary education in Saudi Arabia, an LLB from Cairo University, an M.A. in international relations from the University of Southern California, and a Ph.D. in international relations from London University.

In 1965, al-Qusaibi joined the University of Riyadh as lecturer of political science. He became dean of the College of Administrative Sciences at the same university in 1971. In 1973, he was appointed director general of the Saudi National Railroad Organization, with a deputy ministerial rank. A year later, he was appointed chairman of the Dammam Port Authority. He joined King Khalid's cabinet in 1975 as minister of industry and electricity.

---

(8) Dr. Muhammad Abdu Yamani, Minister of Information:

Was born in 1939 in Mecca. Received his elementary and secondary education in Saudi Arabia. Obtained a B.Sc. in geology from the University of Riyadh, and a Ph.D. in the same field from Cornell University.

Between 1972 and 1973, Yamani lectured at the University of Riyadh; in 1973, he became deputy minister of education; in 1974-1975, he served as rector of the University of King Abd al-Aziz, and he joined King Khalid's cabinet in 1975.

---

(9) Ibrahim Ibn Muhammad Ibn Ibrahim Al Shaykh, Minister of Justice: Traditional education

---

(10) Ibrahim al-Anqari, Minister of Labor and Social Affairs:

Received his elementary and secondary education in Saudi Arabia, and a B.A. from Cairo University. From 1950 to 1974 he served as director of the Bureau of the Minister of Education, as a diplomat at the Saudi Embassy in Washington, D.C., as director general of the Ministry of Interior, and as minister of information in King Faisal's cabinet.

(Table 5.8 continues)

(11) Ahmad Zaki Yamani, Minister of Petroleum and Mineral Resources:

Was born in Dammam in 1938. Received his elementary and secondary education in Saudi Arabia. Obtained an LLB from Cairo University and an LLM from Harvard University.

In his Islamic Law and Contemporary Issues (Karachi: Elite Publishers, 1958), Yamani noted that there is no contradiction between the shari'ah and modern situations. Indeed, Yamani asserted, progress and development will be attained only through the application of the shari'ah. Reflecting the views of Ibn al-Qayyim al-Jawziyah, a noted Hanbali jurist, Yamani suggested that the shari'ah is a system based on the welfare of the individual in the community, both in his everyday life and in anticipation of the life thereafter. The shari'ah, Yamani continued, "is all justice, all compassion, all benefits, and all wisdom." Ahmad Zaki Yamani, Islamic Law and Contemporary Issues (Karachi: Elite Publishers, 1958), pp. 9-10.

(12) Shaykh Abd al-Wahhab Abd al-Wasi', Minister of Pilgrimage Affairs and Awqaf: Traditional education.

(13) Hisham Nazir, Minister of Planning:

Was born in Jeddah in 1932. Received his elementary education in Saudi Arabia; completed his secondary education at Alexandria's Victoria College. In 1957 Nazir received a B.A. in international relations from the University of California and an M.A. in political science from UCLA in 1958.

In 1959 Nazir joined the Directorate General of Oil and Mineral Affairs as an adviser. In 1960 he was appointed director general of the Ministry. In 1968 he became president of the Central Planning Organization, and in 1971 he was appointed as a member of the Council of Ministers by King Faisal. He joined Khalid's cabinet in 1975.

Describing Nazir, Peter Hobday wrote that "[he] has absorbed the American fascination with the 'numbers approach' to everything. As long as the computer says that it can work, and as long as the numbers add up, there is little point in trying to imagine all the reasons why something will not happen" (Peter Hobday, Saudi Arabia Today [London: Macmillan Publishers, 1978], p. 79). Nazir, however, sees no contradiction between Islam and modernity. On the contrary, economic development should be attained and harnessed to serve the Islamic community. Moreover, Nazir is willing to benefit from foreign advisers. The best known of his foreign adviser teams is the Stanford Research Institute of California, which was partially involved in the drafting of the first and second Saudi five year development plans.

(14) Dr. Alawi Darwish Kayal, Minister of Post, Telegraph, and Telephone:

Was born in Jeddah in 1932. Received his elementary and secondary education in Saudi Arabia; obtained a Ph.D. in political science from the United States. From 1959 to 1970 he served as director general of post and as minister of post, telegraph, and telephone in Faisal's cabinet. He retained the same position in King Khalid's 1975 cabinet.

(Table 5.8 continues)

(15) Muhammad Ibrahim Mas'ud, Minister of State Without Portfolio:

Was born in Jeddah in 1919. Received elementary and secondary education in Saudi Arabia and a B. Com. from the Lebanese National University.

In 1936-1937, Mas'ud taught in al-Falah School in Jeddah; in 1941 he was appointed head of a section in the Department of Minerals and Public Works; from 1943 to 1948, he headed the Provisions Department, Ministry of Finance; from 1958 to 1959, he became Minister Plenipotentiary and Inspector of the Diplomatic and Consular Corps, Ministry of Foreign Affairs; from 1959 to 1961, he was Minister Plenipotentiary at the Saudi Embassy, Baghdad, Iraq; from 1961 to 1968, he served as ambassador, and from 1968 to 1975, as deputy foreign minister. He joined King Khalid's cabinet in 1975.

---

(16) Dr. Abd Allah Muhammad al-Omran, Minister of State Without Portfolio:

Was born in 1935. Received his elementary and secondary education in Saudi Arabia and a Ph.D. in law from the United States.

Served as legal adviser to the Council of Ministers between 1970 and 1975; was appointed Minister Without Portfolio in 1975.

---

(17) Dr. Muhammad Abd al-Latif al-Mulhim, Minister of State Without Portfolio:

Was born in 1936. Received his elementary and secondary edication in Saudi Arabia, and an M.A. and Ph.D. in business administration from the United States.

Prior to 1975, he lectured at the University of Riyadh and was dean of the College of Administrative Sciences at the same university.

---

rationalizes the type and direction of planning that his ministry introduces in religious terms. For instance, the Second Five Year Plan, which was introduced in July 9, 1975, provided for the maintenance of a high rate of economic growth, maximization of oil earnings, reduction of economic dependence on the export of crude oil, development of human resources, and creation of a physical infrastructure to support the objectives of the plan. All these objectives are to be attained, "God willing, within an Islamic framework," to enhance the "capability and welfare of Muslims."[15] Another secular-educated minister, Shaykh Ahmad Zaki al-Yamani, reaffirmed this tendency by noting that the development of the material well-being of Muslims should be the objective of government, for the *shari'ah* is "a system based on the welfare of the individual in the community, both in his everyday life and in anticipation of the life thereafter."[16]

Although religious symbolism continues to constitute an important reference point among cabinet members, the same cannot be said of the relatively more junior officials. In a survey of the social attitudes and career preference of 271 key secular-educated and traditionally educated Saudi civil servants, the importance of the religious profession ranked poorly. The respondents were asked in 1970 to rank eleven occupations according to their anticipated returns in terms of happiness

TABLE 5.9
Ranking of Career Preferences[18]

Occupation	Number	Percentage
Doctor	113	42
Businessman	41	15
Alem	26	9
Government Bureau Chief	22	8
Landlord	20	7
Engineer	19	7
Peasant	19	7
Judge	5	2
Small Merchant	3	1.5
Laborer	1	0.5
Imam	1	0.5
Undecided	1	0.5
Total	271	100

and social respectability. As indicated in Table 5.9, government service as well as the religious profession were ranked below physicians and businessmen. Next to physicians (42 percent), the respondents ranked businessmen as a highly prestigious category (15 percent), followed by alem (9 percent) and government officials (8 percent). While the profession of alem was viewed as socially prestigious and desirable by 9 percent of the respondents, only 0.5 percent believed the profession of imam (leader of prayers and administrator of mosque) to be personally rewarding and socially prestigious.[17]

The decline in the prestige of the religious profession as projected in the low ranking of the professions of judge, imam, and alem was not accompanied by the erosion of parochial and traditional values and attitudes. Objective considerations are of little importance in determining the selection of civil servants and in ensuring the necessary cooperation within the organization or among government agencies. It is common, for example, for friends and relatives of key officials to be recruited to the official's department or ministry. Identification of public offices with the private properties of the official heading them is an accepted and expected practice. The results of Awaji's questionnaire disclosed that 45 percent of the respondents had friends and/or relatives who had worked in their agencies before assuming their position. Moreover, 31 percent of the respondents admitted having their closest friends working in the same department or agency.[19]

Another prevalent parochial phenomenon in the Saudi administrative system reflecting the patrimonial character of the polity is that one or two personalities may attract a social clique in the same organization. A clique's activities may extend from personal interaction and cooperation in the inter- or intradepartmental arena to social gatherings and activities. Sixty-six percent of Awaji's respondents noted that personal relationships based on social or regional considerations are likely to motivate a strong esprit de corps among civil servants.[20] In contrast, only 32 percent felt that objective and professional considerations are the primary incentive in achieving a higher degree of cooperation.[21]

The study of the social attitude and behavior of senior civil servants has demonstrated that despite the creation of modern institutions, parochial attitudes prevail.[22] Although traditional values have continued to exist, however, the prestige and activities of the religious profession have declined. This decline may be attributed to two factors: First, it reflects the policy of limiting the role of the religious establishment in the newly created institutions and, by implication, the decline of the religious profession as a vehicle for social mobility. Second, it reflects the overall decline in the social status of the ulama and the religious profession.

Conclusion

Despite the expansion of government jurisdiction and the increase in role differentiation, the patrimonial character of the Saudi polity remains unchanged. The king is the locus of authority. The direction of political activities is decided by him personally, with the aid of senior royal family members and a complex bureaucratic structure. Because of its large size and willingness to adapt to changing demands, the royal family has been able to maintain its traditional role. Senior members of the family are in control of major cabinet portfolios, and the numerous children and grandchildren of Ibn Saud control the more junior positions that ensure continuity. In recognition of the needs generated by the creation of modern administrative institutions, the younger generation of Al Saud, exemplified by the children of King Faisal, have attained secular and specialized education and skills. Religion and religious instruction no longer constitute the educational background required by members of the family in order to maintain their prominence.

The introduction of secular education should not be viewed as precipitating radical changes in the regime's sociopolitical values. On the contrary, there is little correlation between secular education and the regime's orientation. Religion continues to be an important source of political legitimacy, and change is rationalized in religious terms.

The preceding survey of senior civil servants has revealed that despite the creation of modern institutions, parochial values and attitudes remain prevalent. The persistence of these values among civil servants is a reflection of the patrimonial rule that dominates the society. The society is an enlarged household; the personal ties that dominate the activities of the royal family are the model for relationships in other social units.

6
The Process of Nation Building
and Its Consequences

The process of nation building and Al Saud's desire to initiate and control change has had profound effects on the role and position of religion in society. These effects have been both functional and dysfunctional in establishing the legitimacy of the regime and its ability to maintain its patrimonial character. The process of change has manifested itself in increased urbanization, literacy, education, and a higher standard of living. The results of these changes are three-fold. First, the government is better able to satisfy emergent needs now that administrative institutions have been created, the educational system has been expanded, and health and social services have increased and become accessible to citizens. Second, traditional culture has been challenged by alien sociopolitical values and relationships. Indeed, Wahhabi puritanism and extreme affluence seem antithetical to each other in present-day Saudi society. Third, emergent groups, such as the workers and the intellectuals, began to demand political participation. Although Saudi workers and intellectuals are limited in number, their demands and activities are a constant reminder of the dilemma of modernization confronting the ruling monarchies.

Noting this dilemma of ruling monarchies, and indeed that of Al Saud, Samuel P. Huntington has suggested that the centralization of power is necessary to the survival of the regime insofar as it promotes social and economic reforms. This centralization made difficult the expansion of the polity and its assimilation of new groups. The participation of these groups in politics could come at the price of the monarchy. "This is the king's dilemma—must he be the victim of his own achievement? . . . What strategies are open to the monarch to avoid regime instability or destruction?"[1]

Generally speaking, nation building consists of two major functions: breaking through and political integration. Breaking through refers to the decisive alteration or destruction of values, structures, and behaviors that are perceived by the elite as threatening and thus must be effectively constrained or eliminated. Political integration, on the other hand, involves the creation of a new political formula, new political institutions, and new patterns of political behavior—a new community based on norms of reciprocity, on shared sentiments, and on mutual recognition—all of which receive some institutional expression. The nature of the breaking through and the character of political integration (i.e., the type of political community that is created) are determined by the particular strategy that the leadership employs.

The strategies of nation building usually employed by the leadership can be classified into two categories: reformism and revolution. Each of these strategies emphasizes different procedures for effecting change. Reformism stresses the values of compromise and bargaining. It is a strategy of muddling through and shifting alliances, whereby the regime's goals emerge, in the fashion of the marketplace, out of conflict among many groups with different aims. When the elite adopts a reformist strategy, it accepts society as it is and provides some guidelines for the process of development. Economic and social development can proceed only at a rate that is acceptable to the major groups in society.

Viewed as an alternative strategy, revolution directly confronts what are conceived to be the obstacles to change and development. The atmosphere of revolutionary strategy is one of crisis and attack. No opposition is tolerated, and the whole state apparatus is controlled by a militant, disciplined party organization, which has the monopoly of power. The objectives of economic development are of the greatest importance in this system, with emphasis on austerity, discipline, and sacrifice.

A reformist strategy, depending as it does on shifting alliances and bargaining, reduces the ability of the leadership to attain its objectives. The need for bargaining creates an atmosphere in which issues can rarely be dealt with decisively. Moreover, a reformist strategy of bargaining and compromise can result in the absence of effective leadership because of commitments to the various groups in society that seriously limit an elite's ability to deploy resources. This limitation is particularly significant in the face of any attempt by the elite to satisfy the demands of major societal groups. As a consequence, the elite would have less flexibility in formulating its policies. The adoption of a reformist strategy may therefore constrain government performance and increase the base of dissatisfaction. Whereas proponents of change seek more radical transformation of society, advocates of the status quo insist on the preservation of the existing situation. Both, however, constitute potential threats to the survival of the regime.

The Initiation of Change

As a consequence of the Saudi rulers' two-pronged policy of engaging Wahhabism as state ideology and instituting limited administrative and social change, the Saudi polity has exhibited tensions and conflict between two groups: (1) the secular-educated Saudis who advocated more socioeconomic and political reforms, and (2) the religiously inspired traditionalists who desired to reaffirm the religious character of the polity. Balancing the tension between the two is the king who converts tension into balance and binds society together "through conflict no less than collaboration."[2]

Ibn Saud and his successors hoped to maintain a viable socioeconomic order based on Wahhabism but one flexible enough to adjust to changing circumstances. They introduced change to accommodate emergent situations but continued to invoke religion as a means to rationalize that change. The first and most elaborate reform program was initiated in 1962 as a result of internal and external pressures. Despite the tremendous increases in oil revenues, King Saud did not introduce any noticeable change into Saudi living conditions. Under these circumstances, Nasser's Arab nationalism and socialism found fertile ground among secular-educated Saudis who advocated secularization of the polity, economic development, and liberalization of the regime. Prince Talal, who spearheaded this group, sought refuge in 1962 in Cairo; from there he demanded the establishment of a Saudi republic.

Whereas the advocates of change demanded republican rule and socioeconomic reforms, the ulama, merchants, and tribal leaders supported the prevailing conditions. To the latter, change meant displacement and the loss of status. The immediate outcome of the interplay between the two groups was Saud's dismissal and Faisal's assumption of power in 1964.[3]

Once he assumed power, Faisal reunited the offices of king and prime minister and acquired the exclusive authority to appoint, dismiss, and accept the resignation of ministers. This concentration of power in the person of the king seemed to be influenced by Faisal's desire to initiate change without having to accommodate conflicting demands. Controlled change was introduced in the 1962 Ten Point Reform Program, which was rationalized in religious terms. Reform was introduced

> in order to achieve a unified system of government based on the principles of the shari'ah. A Basic Law will be promulgated, drawn from the Quran, the traditions of the Prophet and the acts of the Orthodox

Caliphs. It will set forth the fundamental principles of government and the relationship between the governor and the governed.[4]

More specifically, Faisal's program stipulated the following:

1. While reaffirming the state's adherence to Islamic law, it promised to issue a Basic Law (i.e., a constitution) and establish a consultative council.
2. It pledged to enact regulations that would establish local governments.
3. It proclaimed independence of the judiciary and promised to establish a supreme judicial council and a ministry of justice.
4. It announced that the judicial council would be composed of twenty members chosen from both secular-educated jurists and the ulama.
5. It promised to reinforce Islamic information and *da'wa*.
6. It proclaimed the reform of the Committees for Commanding the Good and Forbidding Evil.
7. It proclaimed the government's concern with developing social welfare policies and pledged control of retail prices, establishment of a scholarship fund for students, social security regulation, a law protecting workers from unemployment, and provision of "innocent" recreational facilities.
8. It announced the intention to regulate economic and commercial activities through appropriate legislation, thus ensuring progress, economic development, and encouragement of capital investment.
9. It pledged a sustained endeavor to develop the country's resources and infrastructure.
10. It abolished slavery in the kingdom.[5]

Although Faisal's program initiated a period of change, it was restricted to the educational and economic spheres, with limited social reforms. On the political front, neither a Basic Law, a consultative assembly, nor local governments were introduced.

Expansion of the Educational System

Educational facilities that existed in the various parts of present-day Saudi Arabia prior to World War I accurately reflected the existing administrative and socioeconomic conditions. In addition to the *kuttab* (elementary *Quranic* schools), the provinces had specialized in teaching circles known as the *halaqa* (circle) in the houses of prominent ulama and in major mosques, as well as several private schools sponsored by individual benefactors such as the al-Falah schools in Mecca and Jeddah.

The organization of formal secular education in the country took place in 1925 when Ibn Saud ordered the creation of the Directorate General of Education. The ulama opposed the introduction of secular education out of the fear that it would damage the fabric of Wahhabi society. Through the persistence of Ibn Saud, however, significant progress took place between 1925 and the year, namely 1953, in which the Directorate General was replaced by the Ministry of Education and headed by Prince Fahd. These developments included the provision of primary and secondary education, teacher training, technical education, a scholarship program for Saudi students to study abroad, and the creation of the first two institutions of higher education, the Faculty of Shari'ah and Teachers' College, both in Mecca.

In 1948 there were only 182 primary schools, with an enrollment of 21,409 students. By 1952, the number had risen to 301 schools, with an enrollment of 39,920 students.[6] In 1960–1962, the Saudi educational system began to experience even more rapid changes. These changes were evident in increasing public expenditures; the number of schools, teachers, student enrollments, and graduations; a new emphasis on technical training and higher education; and women's education. With respect to public expenditure, only S.R. 168.8 million ($45 million) were allocated for education in 1960–1961, whereas the amount reached S.R. 523.9 million ($145.5 million) in 1967–1968 and S.R. 1,265.6 million ($361.6 million) in 1974–1975.[7]

Other evidence of the growing emphasis on education is seen in the increasing size of school enrollments. In 1960, for example, 115,000 students registered at the primary level; 9,500 at the elementary general; 2,000 at the intermediary vocational level; 3,500 at the level of secondary-teacher training; and 1,300 at the college and university levels.[8] In addition, 200 schools were built to accommodate the overall increase.[9]

Based on the religious character of the society, and consistent with Al Saud's justification of change in religious terms, Saudi educational planners indicate that

> the purpose of education is to have the students understand Islam in a correct and comprehensive manner, to plant and spread the Islamic creed, to furnish the student with the values, teachings and ideals of Islam, to equip him with various skills and knowledge, to develop his conduct in constructive directions, [and] to develop the society economically, socially and culturally.[10]

The same objectives were reiterated in the Second Five Year Plan (1975–1980), which stressed "maintaining the religious and moral values of Islam over developing human resources."[11]

While religious influence on education may be relatively easy to maintain at the primary and even secondary levels, it is more difficult to do so at the secondary or higher levels. Religious subjects cannot dominate the curricula of secular colleges, and students cannot be monitored at all times when they study abroad. An examination of Saudi universities and colleges shows that developing human resources is the most important goal of the government and that the number of students enrolled in religious programs is less than those in secular institutions.[12] The main secular institutions in the country are Riyadh University (1957); King Abd al-Aziz University, with faculties at both Jeddah and Mecca (1967); the Islamic University of Imam Muhammad Ibn Saud, at Riyadh (1974); King Faisal University, at Dammam and Hufuf (1975); and the University of Petroleum and Minerals (UPM), at Dhahran (1975). Although these universities, with the exception of UPM, offer degrees in *shari'ah* and religious studies, their main emphasis is on human resources development. They had a total enrollment of more than 24,000 students during 1979–1980. The main religious university in the country is the Islamic University of Medina, which had an enrollment of about 380 students during the same period. There are other institutions of religious studies that offer courses in *da'wa* (preaching), *shari'ah*, and *Quranic* studies, but enrollment remains low. In addition to the 24,000 students in the country, it is necessary to note that there are at present more than 13,000 government-sponsored students at American universities.[13] The topics they study range from computer science and engineering to nutrition and police technology. Only a limited number of them study Islamic subjects. For example, of 280 Saudi students in the United States during the academic year 1979–1980, only 7 were registered in Islamic studies.[14]

Although the ulama have opposed education for women, Saudi educational planners introduced such education in 1960. Education for women prior to 1960 was available only in the larger cities of Jeddah, Medina, Mecca, and Riyadh. Girls received education from private female tutors or in the *kuttab*, where a small number of girls would attend classes given by a female instructor to memorize parts of the *Quran* and solve simple mathematical problems. Wealthy families would employ private tutors who lived with the family and who in many cases acted not only as teachers and advisers but also as nurses and companions to the children.

A few private and more secular female elementary schools also existed in the Hejaz region, some of which followed the curricula of the Ministry of Education while others developed their own curricula. Overall, there were many who did not accept the education of girls, considering it conducive instead to the degradation and immorality of women and to their revolt against the traditions of society.

The official recognition of women's right to formal education was granted in 1959 when a royal speech was delivered stating that a decision had been made to open government schools for girls under the control of a committee to be responsible to the Grand Mufti.[15] The placement of female education under ulama control was a necessary measure to secure their approval. A year later, the General Presidency of the Schools of Girls was created. This body is effectively a ministry, governed by a shaykh with the same powers, privileges, and status as those of a minister.

The expansion of female primary and secondary education ultimately led to the creation of college and university facilities for women. In 1960–1961, only 4 women were enrolled in evening classes at Riyadh University. Five years later, this number increased to 118 students. Moreover, at Riyadh University female undergraduates may study at home and take degrees in arts or sciences. King Abd al-Aziz University in Jeddah offers arts and science courses, and the same university has a campus in Mecca that offers courses in the arts and the *shari'ah.* Where female instructors are not available, as is most often the case, and because women are not allowed to mingle with men, closed circuit television is used to broadcast lectures given by male professors.

Despite the expansion of female education, the object of such education nonetheless remains to bring her up "in a sound Islamic way so that she can fulfill her role in life as a successful housewife, ideal wife and good mother, and to prepare her for other activities that suit her nature such as teaching, nursing and the medical profession."[16] Moreover, Saudi educational policy stipulates that co-education is prohibited in all stages of education except at the nursery level.

The educational policies stated by the Saudis reflect the government's desire to develop materially and yet retain Wahhabism as the guiding ideology, to create a young generation of Wahhabis versed in Islam and Wahhabi fundamentalism as well as engineering and computer science. But the reality of the situation points to an erosion of religious education and the increase in the number of secular schools. The political implications of the increase of secular-educated Saudis are two-fold: First, this group's desire for greater political participation will exert pressure on the political system and may eventually alter the regime's patrimonial character. Second, the growing population of secular-educated Saudis means an emerging "world view" at variance with that of their elders and the ulama. Consequently, their role in government and society will heighten tension and conflict between them and the traditionalists.

Socioeconomic Process

The oil revenues that in the 1950s began to change the country's relatively poor and isolated society had, by the middle 1970s, increased tremendously: $0.6 billion in 1965 to $1.2 billion in 1970 and $4.3 billion in 1973. In 1974, these revenues increased to $22.5 billion as a result of price quadrupling in the aftermath of the Ramadan War. In 1977, oil revenues reached $37 billion, nearly doubled again to about $70 billion in 1979 following Khomeini's revolution, and reached $90 billion in 1980.[17]

As the leader in oil production and revenues, and because of the royal family's desire to introduce socioeconomic change and control its direction, the country embarked on the most ambitious development and public expenditure program in the Arab world. The Second Five Year Plan (1975–1980) called for an expenditure of $145 billion. The Third Five Year Plan (1980–1985) is budgeted at $250–$300 billion.[18]

Government planning and expenditures had a profound impact on Saudi society. Until the 1940s, the country had a pastoral economy based on the raising of goats, sheep, and camels. The majority of the urban population lived in small villages built of mudbrick and earned a living from subsistence agriculture. With the exception of the oil sector no industrial activity existed, but trade was an important activity in urban centers. In the cities of Mecca, Medina, and Jeddah pilgrimage constituted a main source of income.

As a result of the tremendous increase in oil revenues beginning in the 1960s, a number of development projects were undertaken to improve the living conditions of Saudis. In the last decade alone, 2,000 villages were provided with electricity; 15,000 kilometers of paved roads were built, 700,000 telephones were installed, and 300,000 housing units were constructed.[19] The number of doctors grew from less than 1,000 to 4,000 within a three-year period. Currently, moreover, two huge industrial complexes are under way in Yanbu and Jubail. The town of Jubail, in particular, will grow with industrial development. It is planned that 100,000 housing units will be constructed to accommodate this growth.

Reflecting the role of religion in rationalizing change, the primary objective stated in the current Five Year Plan is the "preservation of religious values and traditions." This objective is followed by those of "improving the welfare and standard of living of Saudis, the preservation of national security, and economic stability."[20] Yet, although material and economic development has been achieved, the consequences of such change have (1) eroded traditional values and (2) threatened the regime's patrimonial character.

Erosion of Traditional Culture

Saudi Arabia has had no colonial experience; indeed, most of its population remained insulated from external cultural influences until the 1940s. The fact that Ibn Saud had to battle the ulama in the 1930s to introduce a secular educational system, the automobile, the radio, and the telephone demonstrates the extent of this early cultural isolation. Recent external cultural influences, however, have penetrated Saudi society in two major forms: expatriates and consumerism.[21] The tremendous increase in the number of foreigners visiting or working in the country and the number of Saudis traveling abroad have eroded traditional culture. In 1979 alone, approximately 2.5 million worked in or visited the kingdom. This number equals about half of the total native Saudi population.[22] As many as 900,000 Saudis traveled abroad in the same year, a figure representing nearly one-fifth of the total population. To illustrate the impact of this travel abroad on traditional culture, we can note that about 15 percent of those taking such trips in 1979 were females. The percentage of females traveling abroad would be of little significance were it not for the fact that Saudi women cannot mingle with men and are mostly confined to their homes. These rules, however, are not observed abroad.[23]

To appreciate the impact of foreign labor on Saudi society, we might note that migrant labor accounted for 43 percent of the total work force in the mid-1970s.[24] As indicated in Table 6.1, within some sectors the migrant labor share of employment is even higher: more than 50 percent in manufacturing, electricity, construction, trade, and finance. The largest sector hiring expatriates is that of construction, which employed about 240,000 in 1975, 85 percent of whom were expatriates. The high percentage of expatriates implies the introduction of alien culture into society. Many Wahhabi prohibitions are not observed by members of this group. Consequently, Ministry of Interior "instructions" are issued regularly to remind foreigners to observe and abide by Saudi culture.

A reflection of the scope of change in Saudi society is the astronomical increase in crime, divorce, alcoholism, and other indicators of social problems. Between 1971 and 1975, the administrative manpower of Saudi prisons more than doubled. It increased from a total of 2,255 policemen and civilians to 5,541, a 146 percent increase in five years. Between 1975 and 1979, the number of crimes officially reported increased by 169 percent. Leading the increase was murder related to honor and vendetta (94 percent), economic and financial crimes (154 percent), and fraud (318 percent). Alcohol and drug offenses as well as other crimes witnessed an even greater increase—

TABLE 6.1
Employment by Economic Sector and Nationality (1975)

Sector	Saudi Arabian No.	%	Non-National No.	%	Total	Saudi Arabians' share of all employment %
Agriculture and fishing	530,700	51.7	54,900	7.1	585,600	90.6
Mining and petroleum	15,400	1.5	11,600	1.5	27,000	57.0
Manufacturing	21,550	2.1	94,350	12.2	115,900	18.6
Electricity, gas, and water	7,200	0.7	13,150	1.7	20,350	35.4
Construction	35,900	3.5	203,400	26.3	239,300	15.0
Wholesale and retail trade	30,600	5.9	131,500	17.0	192,100	31.5
Transport, storage, and communication	72,900	7.1	30,950	4.0	103,850	70.2
Finance and insurance	5,150	0.5	6,950	0.9	12,100	42.6
Community and personal services	277,100	27.0	226,600	29.3	503,700	55.0
TOTAL	1,026,500	100.0	773,400	100.0	1,799,900	57.0

Source: Saudi Arabia, Population Census 1974, vols. 1-14 (Dammam: Ministry of Finance and National Planning, Central Department of Statistics). Also cited in J. Birks and C. Sinclair, International Migration and Development in the Arab Region (Geneva: ILO, 1980), pp. 159-160, and in Saad Eddin Ibrahim, The New Arab Social Order (Boulder, Colorado: Westview Press, 1982), p. 96.

1,400 percent by 1979. Reported "moral" (i.e. sexual) crimes increased 150.5 percent during the same period.[25]

Although most of those convicted are Saudis, foreigners account for more than 40 percent of the crimes, 45 percent of which are financial and fraud cases. Another indicator of the erosion of traditional values is the growing discrepancy between publicly sanctioned mores and privately practiced behavior. Although public theatres are still prohibited by law, private cinema and video clubs are common; although Wahhabism prohibits cigarette smoking, tobacco is subject to government taxation; and although photography is prohibited by Wahhabi teachings, photography stores are widespread.

Secular and Religious Opposition to Change

Because of Al Saud's reformist policy of advocating material change while retaining Wahhabism, the reaction to government-initiated change manifested itself through two groups: the secularists and the fundamentalists. Both advocated a distinct program calling for the abolition of monarchical rule.

Secular Opposition

Labor. The first political challenge that confronted Al Saud's rule following the unification of the kingdom in 1932 came from ARAMCO workers striking in 1953 and 1956. The significance of the two strikes must be viewed in the light of government regulations concerning labor, especially the "Labour and Workmen Regulations Act" of October 10, 1947. This act included sixty articles that regulated labor activities. Its most important provision was prohibition of the creation of labor unions and labor assemblies and introduction of the work permit.[26]

The early signs of labor protest surfaced in the summer of 1953 when a workers' committee was organized in Dhahran. This committee claimed to represent 6,500 ARAMCO workers, whose demands were for increased social services and higher wages. Committee members requested the right to form a union from Crown Prince Saud in 1953. Their petition was rejected. Workers' spokesmen were jailed, and a royal commission was established to investigate the reasons behind the workers' request to form a union.

The imprisonment of the workers' leaders transformed the initial request to unionize into a labor protest with a specific cause and a ready-made set of martyrs. Their arrest precipitated the strike of 13,000 ARAMCO employees in Dhahran, Abqaiq, and Ras Tanura, all vital oil areas. To counter the strike, armed troops were sent to the Eastern Province, and Crown Prince Saud ordered the strikers to return to work under the penalty of dismissal. Continued defiance by the workers of the return-to-work order precipitated more arrests. In the end, however, the workers complied and returned to work.

What did ARAMCO workers gain? What was the significance of the strike? Although no formal concessions were made, the strike, which was the first in the kingdom's history, had two implications: (1) ARAMCO introduced immediate socioeconomic reforms: a housing program for workers; an increase in the minimum daily wages; improvement of promotion policies; restoration of food and clothing subsidies; construction of the first school for the workers' children; shortening of the work week; and a Communication Committee, which was established as a channel between workers and management. (2) Due to the imprisonment of its leaders, the strike was transformed from a purely industrial dispute into a challenge to the established political order.

Although the 1953 ARAMCO strike was motivated primarily by economic factors, the 1956 strike was caused by the increasing trend toward Arab nationalism. This latter strike occurred during King Saud's visit to Dhahran on June 9, 1956. The protesters made no economic demands, nor did they express any overt criticism of the government. Rather, they "displayed nationalist and anti-imperialist sentiment."[27] The Saudi government reaction was immediate and repressive. Strike leaders were imprisoned, and an ultimatum was issued that demanded an immediate return to work. The Labour and Workmen Regulations of 1947 were supplemented on June 11, 1956, by a royal decree outlawing strikes under the penalty of imprisonment.

With the arrest of labor leaders in 1956 and the imposition of restrictions on labor assemblies, and because the majority of the work force is now expatriate, labor activism has subsided.

Liberals in the Royal Family. The liberal faction, headed by Prince Talal, King Saud's younger brother, and including in its membership four junior princes, proposed a draft constitution and the formation of a legislative assembly in 1962. In his capacity as prime minister, Faisal rejected this demand; yet his rejection seemed to create the conditions for a temporary alliance between King Saud and Talal. With the resignation of Faisal Saud immediately formed a new Council of Ministers, naming himself prime minister and assigning the ministerial posts of finance and national economy to Prince Talal and the newly created ministry of Petroleum and Mineral Resources to Abd Allah al-Tariki, an Arab nationalist. King Saud's ploy of manipulating the liberals soon became apparent as he found himself at odds with their demands to establish an elected national council to draft a constitution. The conflict between Saud and Talal was further intensified as Talal began publicly to criticize Saud's rule, an act that led to his dismissal from the Council of Ministers. Talal relinquished his royal title and in 1962 sought refuge in Cairo, where he formed a committee for "the liberation of Saudi Arabia." This committee was extremely weak and did not pose any serious threat to the regime's survival. It lacked both mass support and a clear ideology. With the decline of Nasserism in the late 1960s, and with Faisal's introduction of reform, Talal returned to the kingdom. He regained his royal status, and is currently engaged in business.

Military Support of the Established Order. The Saudi military has been an important factor of support for the royal family. To understand its role, we must inquire into the relationship between the military and society. Both the internal organization and the external environment are important in this context because organizations such as the military have a momentum of their own while at the same time existing in and responding to the society at large. In other words, the Saudi military organization, however independent, nevertheless reflects the economic, political, and social activities in the society.

In contrast to the majority of Arab armies, however, the Saudi military establishment has not traditionally played any significant role in politics. Following the brief Saudi-Yemeni confrontation in 1934, when Ibn Saud annexed Najran, the Saudi army was reduced to a minimum. In 1948, Ibn Saud allowed the United States to use military base facilities at Dhahran, where ARAMCO is located, in return for American training of the nascent Saudi air force. In 1951, the United States Training Mission was established, replacing an earlier British training mission.

The desire of Al Saud to modernize the military and control its activities is greatly influenced by two considerations: (1) the royal family is acutely aware that military establishments in the Arab world have acted as a destabilizing force; and (2) to protect its vast oil resources, the country must organize and train an effective, modern military establishment.[28] The need for a modern military establishment was realized first during the 1962–1970 Yemen War, and again as a result of the 1967 Arab-Israeli War. The Yemen War demonstrated the impotency of the Saudi military in confronting the Egyptian-sponsored Republican army; the 1967 Arab-Israeli War impressed upon Al Saud that Saudi participation in any subsequent Arab-Israeli confrontation would be a necessity for both domestic and Arab considerations. In addition, the 1968 British withdrawal from the Gulf area created a power vacuum that the Saudis realized was urgently in need of filling.

Consequently, the Saudi political elite commenced the expansion and modernization of the military. The current strength of the armed forces is 53,000, of whom 34,500 are in the army, 17,000 in the air force, and 1,500 in the navy.[29] Actual defense expenditures quadrupled between 1973 and 1974, from $1,438 million to $6,771 million, representing a per capita expenditure of $1,692 (as calculated on the basis of a population estimate of 4 million). There is no indication of expenditure reduction in the 1980s. If the 1980–1982 purchase orders are any indication, military expenditures may even rise. In 1980, for example, Saudi Arabia signed a $3.5 billion contract with France for the purchase of warships, supplyships, coastal defense equipment, and helicopters for naval warfare.[30]

Although the Saudi military is generally supportive of Al Saud, a number of attempted coups have taken place. In 1945, Abd Allah al-Mandeli, an air force pilot, attempted to bomb Ibn Saud's encampment at Mount Arafat. He missed the target and was arrested and executed. A number of air force pilots were also arrested on suspicion of conspiracy to assassinate King Saud following the July 14, 1958, Iraqi revolution. In 1962, six officers were jailed for communicating with the Liberal Princes faction in Cairo; in 1969, an attempted coup was uncovered, and 100 military personnel were arrested;[31] and in 1977, a number of army officers were court-martialed for their role in an attempted coup.[32]

To avoid the potential threat of the military, Al Saud has adopted a two-fold policy. First, the National Guard is separated from the armed forces and is under the command of Crown Prince Abd Allah, a brother of King Fahd. The Guard acts as a counterforce to the regular armed forces. It is a paramilitary force composed of 20,000 regulars and irregulars, with a sophisticated light and heavy arsenal. A key feature of the Guard is its tribal structure. All Guard recruits are of tribal background, and battalions are structured on a tribal basis. In addition to its role in countering the armed forces, the National Guard has an internal security function, especially in oil-producing areas. It acts as an internal security deterrent against any potential uprising.

The second policy adopted by Al Saud to neutralize the potential threat of the military is one involving financial rewards. Saudi enlisted personnel receive financial incentives to join the military. Enlisted men are given land and financial assistance to construct a house; officers are granted additional land and interest-free loans for investment purposes. Moreover, military personnel pay rates were doubled in 1981—for a lieutenant up to $2,445 a month, and for a general up to $6,420.

The Saudi military is a newly created organization that has no tradition of its own, nor can it claim national liberation victories. It was Ibn Saud who mobilized the bedouins and led them to victory. In addition to its recent creation, the military is not politicized. It is closely identified with Al Saud, and the government policy of co-optation makes it an obvious beneficiary of the regime. Although there were a number of reported attempted coups, these were isolated incidents. The military is supportive of Al Saud and it is unlikely to pose any threat to the regime's stability.

The Intellectuals. The prominence of intellectuals in the politics of developing areas may be attributed to their role in articulating nationalist sentiment and the sense of direction and purpose instilled in their countrymen. "They created the political life of the underdeveloped countries; they have been its instigators, its leaders, and its executants."[33] This group includes "all persons with an advanced modern education and the intellectual concerns and skills ordinarily associated with it."[34] It is highly politicized and plays a vital role in shaping national politics.

Since Saudi Arabia was not subjected to any form of colonialism, and because of the recent character of the educational system, Saudi intellectuals have played little role in national politics. Although a number of underground opposition movements exist, they are rudimentary and weak. Most of their members are students in foreign countries, many of whom sever ties upon returning to the kingdom. This may be attributed to the political system's ability to integrate and satisfy the material needs of this group, as well as to the effectiveness of Saudi internal security forces.

In 1956, a number of Saudi communists and former members of the Workers' Committee established the National Reform Front (NRF). Two years later, the communist element within the NRF seceded and created their own National Liberation Front (NLF). Its objective was to introduce

far reaching change in all aspects of Saudi Arabian life. We are for a state system that would speak for the people's interests and pursue a policy against imperialism, Zionism, and reaction. We demand a democratic constitution ensuring basic rights, including the right to set up political parties, trade unions and other mass public organizations, the right to strike, hold demonstrations, meetings, etc. . . . We demand the dismantling of all foreign bases in our country and the abrogation of the shackling military agreements forced on it. The Front also wants revision of existing concession contracts with foreign oil monopolies to provide for the principle of broad state participation in the entire process from prospecting to marketing. . . . The nation is in urgent need of a public sector of the economy. The Front stands for extensive political relations and close economic and cultural cooperation with the Soviet Union and all countries of the socialist community.[35]

In late 1975, the National Liberation Front changed its name to the Saudi Arabian Communist party. It has a small membership, not exceeding thirty, and is ineffective. Another opposition group, active in the 1960s but no longer operative, is the Union of People of the Arabian Peninsula (UPAP), a Nasserist organization led by Naser Sa'id. The UPAP manifested itself through the issuance of statements condemning Saudi rule.[36]

A more active and better organized opposition group is the Saudi branch of the Baath party. It was created in 1958, and in 1963 became the largest opposition group. Following the split between the Syrian and Iraqi Baath in the mid-1960s, many members left the organization altogether, while others followed the Iraqi line. The pro-Iraqi faction is most active among Saudi students in the United States. In addition to *Saut al-Tali'a,* a regular journal since 1978, this group publishes pamphlets and studies critical of Al Saud. A review of the literature shows the group's inability to present a cohesive ideology. In the pamphlets, and in an interview with three Tali'a members in the United States, there is no evidence of an ideological program.[37]

A more radical Saudi opposition group is the Popular Democratic party (PDP), which was created in 1970 and includes in its membership Marxists and Arab nationalists. The PDP advocates Marxist economic policy as well as armed struggle to "liberate" not only the Arabian Peninsula but the whole of the Arab world. In 1971, the Popular Struggle Front split from the Popular Democratic Party. It publishes *al-Nidal,* and its activity is limited to this publication.[38]

All the aforementioned organizations are weak and their political role is insignificant. Most of their members are students in the United States or in Arab countries, but some withdraw once they return to the kingdom. Despite ideological differences among these organizations, they advocate the abolition of monarchical rule and the introduction of some variation of a socialist order. The views of these groups are best expressed by a statement issued by the Saudi Council for Solidarity and Peace. In September 26, 1977, *Tariq al-Sha'b,* the council's newspaper, presented a number of points condemning Saudi rule:

Fahd failed to implement the promise, made following King Faisal's assassination in 1975, to establish a consultative assembly; government liberalization policy is symbolic; some political prisoners were released following Faisal's assassination, but a¹campaign of arrests and political liquidation of opponents was initiated in 1977. We demand the promulgation of a constitution, the creation of political parties, trade union, and social and cultural organizations. We also demand the nationalization of Saudi oil.³⁹

Religious Opposition

Although religion legitimates Al Saud's rule, religious opposition began to emerge in recent years, demanding the overthrow of Saudi rule and the creation of a "genuinely Islamic republic." Two groups are of importance: the Organization of the Islamic Revolution and the neo-Ikhwan. The first, which was founded in the late 1970s, derives financial support from Iran. Its membership is confined to Shi'i Saudis. It follows Khomeini's vision of Islamic rule. In *The Word of People,* a pamphlet distributed by members of the organization during the pilgrimage season of 1981 in Mecca, the organization outlined its objectives:

In the name of Allah:

As the time when the Muslim ummah is turning to real Islam as the only hope for progress, freedom and complete independence, the ummah faces a dangerous enemy represented by ruling regimes of the so-called Islamic states. The Saudi family is one of these regimes. . . . Their regime is the most dangerous enemy of Islam because they use the cover of religion to legitimate their otherwise unIslamic rule. . . . Ask yourselves: does Islam allow a royal family to have luxurious palaces and share in commercial firms?

We demand: (1) an immediate end to the wave of indiscriminate arrests in Qatif and Ahsa [both are Shi'i regions], and the release of all political prisoners—especially those arrested in the Eastern province while practising religious rites of Ashoora. (2) we deplore the dictatorship of Al Saud and demand that an Islamic constitution be introduced to secure democracy and progress for people. (3) our Muslim people in the Arabian Peninsula are one people, regardless of sect, condemning the regime's sectarian policy of inciting Sunnis against Shi'is. (4) we demand a cutdown in the rate of oil production. (5) we demand social justice to end mass poverty. (6) we demand the abolition of all treaties signed with the United States.⁴⁰

Because of this movement's link with Iran and its representation of Shi'i interests in Saudi Arabia, its activities remain rudimentary and its following is limited.

The Neo-Ikhwan: Religious Opposition in Action

On November 20, 1979, the Grand Mosque of Mecca was seized by a group of fundamentalists who denounced the Saudi regime and proclaimed the appearance of a Mahdi (redeemer). Both then Crown Prince Fahd and Prince Abd Allah, commander of the National Guard, were out of the country at the time. The Saudi government was ill-prepared to face this type of insurrection. It was not an attack against government offices, army barracks, or radio and television stations, such that government could act swiftly to eliminate the attackers. Nor was it a foreign-inspired movement to be dismissed as such and eliminated with ease. Rather, it was an Islamic uprising in protest of what its members described as the religious and moral laxity and degeneration of Saudi rulers, and advocating the revival of seventh-century Islamic society.

The seizure of the mosque underscored the existence of three deeply rooted problems concerning the relationship between religion and state in the kingdom: (1) how to reconcile sudden and immense wealth as well as rapid modernization with adherence to eighteenth-century Wahhabism; (2) the fact that religious fundamentalism and royal politics are not always compatible; and (3) the vulnerability of the royal family to attack from religious fundamentalists as well as secular elements within the society. A study of the identity of the rebels and of their ideology and objectives will demonstrate Al Saud's dilemma with respect to the maintenance of religion as state ideology while fostering material development.

Background

The organizer, military leader, and theoretician of the neo-Ikhwan movement was Juhaiman al-Utaiby, a former member of the National Guard and student of theology at the Mecca Islamic University.[41] The proclaimed Mahdi, Muhammad Ibn Abd Allah al-Qahtani, was a former theology student of Shaykh Abd al-Aziz al-Baz, head of the Higher Council of Ifta' and Research. Before joining Shaykh al-Baz's religious studies circle in the early 1970s, al-Qahtani worked at Riyadh Shumaysi Central Hospital, was accused of theft, and then was imprisoned for a brief period. Following his release, he became extremely religious and joined the Islamic University, where he met Juhaiman. In 1979, he married Juhaiman's sister.

The exact number of the insurgents remains unknown. It is estimated, however, to be around four hundred.[42] From the sixty-three who were publicly executed, it is possible to ascertain that the majority were Saudi Najdis in their early and mid-thirties. Among the non-

Saudis, there were ten Egyptians, six South Yemenis, one North Yemeni, three Kuwaitis, one Sudanese, and one Iraqi.[43]

As for the insurgents' social background, little information is available. Based on the social background of the movement's leaders and interviews with two imams at the Grand Mosque in Mecca who claim to have known Juhaiman, it may be noted that some were unemployed whereas others worked for shopkeepers or were full-time students at Mecca University.[44]

Financial Support and Military Training. The insurgents apparently received their financial support from within the kingdom. Three sources are suggested. As theology students and "pious Muslims," aside from attending public prayers and participating in discussion groups, they raised funds through the selling of religious pamphlets and soliciting donations.[45] A second source is suggested by *Saut al-Tali'a,* namely, that the insurgents received aid from dissidents in the military, the religious establishment, and even members of the royal family.[46] This assertion remains unsubstantiated, however. Finally, as noted by David Holden and Richard Johns, the son of a wealthy Jeddah merchant, Yusuf Bajunaid, sold a property in Jeddah to cover the cost of weapons.[47]

Financial assistance aside, the actual acquisition of arms posed no difficulty for the insurgents. Three possible sources helped them to obtain weapons: (1) As members of a tribal society that takes pride in the possession of arms and hunting, most Saudis own weapons. Prior to the insurrection, there was little restriction on the possession or movement of arms, and arms trade was a flourishing business in the kingdom. (2) The smuggling of arms from Syria, Jordan, and Iraq facilitated the acquisition of weapons.[48] (3) The insurgents attacked a National Guard base near Jeddah and stole light weapons.[49]

Objectives and Ideology. The objectives of the insurgents were clearly stated in the writings of Juhaiman and the lengthy pronouncements made over loudspeakers during the seizure of the mosque. These writings and pronouncements reveal the ideological aspect of the movement and enable us to ascertain how the insurgents justified the seizure, the timing of their attack, and the choice of Muhammad Ibn Abd Allah al-Qahtani as their Mahdi.

Seven pamphlets are known to have been written by Juhaiman. These pamphlets dealt with theological questions, presented a summary of two works by Ibn Taymiyah, denounced the rule of Al Saud, and condemned the state ulama for their collaboration with Al Saud. The central feature of the insurgents' ideology is the reconstruction of an Islamic society as it was known in seventh-century Arabia; in other words, the revival of the society is to be achieved through the Mahdi. Juhaiman quoted a *hadith* attributed to the Prophet Muhammad that viewed the Muslim history as a degeneration of political authority from Prophethood, the caliphate, illegitimate kingship, tyrannical kingship, and finally a return to the caliphate. The movement from one period to another is decided by God, and the Mahdi will appear at the end of the period of tyrannical kingship and govern with justice and compassion.

Juhaiman and his followers seized the mosque not in the manner of a modern insurrectionary movement, but with a fantastic dream of restoring a purified order to "corrupt Arabia." They rationalized their seizure by means of a *hadith* that suggests that the Mahdi will appear at the Ka'ba at the turn of an Islamic century in the period of tyrannical kingship.[50] They also believed that once the Mahdi appears all Muslims will pay him allegiance, whereas the unbelievers' army will vanish. Again, based on the *hadith* that Juhaiman attributed to the Prophet Muhammad and read numerous times during the seizure, ". . . the earth would open to engulf the army of unbelievers who will come to dislodge the Mahdi."

As for the choice of the Mahdi, the insurgents claimed that Muhammad Ibn Abd Allah al-Qahtani met the name requirement and exhibited the physical attributes specified by Muhammad the Prophet in his description of the Mahdi. (Others have claimed that al-Quraishi meets these criteria.) "The Mahdi is from me," the Prophet noted; "he has a wide forehead, a hooked nose, and will fill the earth with justice and equity as it had been filled with injustice and tyranny." Another *hadith* noted that "even if only one day were to remain to the Day of Judgment, God will lengthen this day until He proclaims a man from my family whose name corresponds with mine, and whose father's name corresponds with mine." It was not surprising, then, that Juhaiman adopted Muhammad Ibn Abd Allah al-Qahtani (or Quraishi), whose name and physical attributes corresponded with those of the Prophet, as the awaited Mahdi.

The writings of Juhaiman and the actions of his followers reflect the confusion and rage that beset many Saudis as a result of the rapid change that took place after the discovery of oil: "Who are we?" asks Juhaiman in his pamphlet *The Ikhwan:*

They slander us from all quarters and tell lies about us. . . . We are Muslims who wanted to learn the Shari'ah and quickly realized that it could not be learned in government controlled institutions. . . . We have broken with the opportunists and bureaucrats. . . . We study the authentic Sunnah and *tafsir al-hadith* without blinded commitment to any certain madhhab.[51]

In another pamphlet entitled *Rulership, Payment of Allegiance, Obedience and the Unveiling of the Ruler's Deception of Commoners and Seekers of Knowledge,* Juhaiman rejected state-run religion and condemned the ulama who are "bought up by a corrupt regime with money and promises of promotion."

Juhaiman's ideology underlines the dilemma confronting Saudi rulers in maintaining eighteenth-century Wahhabism as state ideology while developing materially. Many of the views presented by Juhaiman concerning the Mahdi and the evolution of Muslim history are similar if not identical to the doctrine of Shaykh Muhammad Ibn Abd al-Wahhab. Prince Nayf described the insurgents as deviants from orthodox Islam (*al-Islam al-sahih*) and lunatics.[52] Reflecting the government's position, Salim al-Lawzi of *al-Hawadith* drew a parallel between the insurgents and the religious fanatics of Jonestown in Guyana.[53] Denying that the insurgents had any political demands or objectives, then Crown Prince Fahd told *al-Safir* that "the insurgents had no demands or objectives other than [those of] the proclaimed Mahdi, and the whole matter does not exceed an empty dream and empty words."[54] A review of the writings of Shaykh Muhammad Ibn Abd al-Wahhab, however, shows his acceptance of the *ahadith* quoted by the insurgents concerning the evolution of Islamic history, the appearance of a Mahdi, and the vanishing of the invader's army. Shaykh Abd al-Wahhab devoted an entire chapter in *Al-Mu'alafat* to the Mahdi and his awaited appearance.[55] This was and is the king's dilemma—how to adapt eighteenth-century Wahhabism to the realities of the twentieth century.

Consequences of the Insurrection. Faced with the insurrection, King Khalid mobilized the support of the state ulama. He convened the Higher Council of Ifta', headed by Shaykh Abd al-Aziz al-Baz, requesting the issuance of *fatwa* supporting Al Saud and authorizing military intervention in the sacred sanctuary. The ulama complied with the king's demand and noted that there would be a Mahdi, but that he would appear with clear signs and in opposition to a corrupt ruler. The Saudi government, they further noted, enforces the dictates of the *shari'ah*, and rebellion against its ruler is treason.[56]

Having secured the ulama's support, Saudi forces managed to dislodge the insurgents on December 3, killing the proclaimed Mahdi in the process and capturing the military leader and theoretician of the movement as well as some one hundred seventy individuals, including women and children.[57]

The seizure of the mosque underlined the government's vulnerability to attacks from religious elements. It underscored Al Saud's dilemma in accommodating traditional Wahhabism to present-day realities. To counter the insurgents' accusation that Al Saud had deviated from orthodox Islam, to moderate militant Wahhabism, and to balance the interests of secular and religious elements in the country, Al Saud adopted a two-fold policy: First, state ulama were instructed to emphasize in their Friday sermons the destructive character of the uprising, the religiosity of Saudi rulers, and the fact that Islam is a religion of moderation (*al-Islam din wassat*). In an interview with imams in Riyadh, the following themes were stressed:

1. Because of Al Saud, Islam has become victorious (*Nasar al-Lah al-Islam bi Al Saud*).
2. Rebellion against rulers is not allowed as long as the ruler enforces the *shari'ah*. Al Saud are Muslim rulers, Guardians of the Holy Places, and thanks to them the country has become prosperous.
3. Islam is the religion of moderation. It rejects fanaticism of all sorts.
4. God gave Saudis oil and wealth. They should enjoy God's rewards in moderation.
5. Those who deprive themselves of enjoying life with moderation are sinful.[58]

The same themes were reiterated by other Saudi ulama. In a survey of the Friday sermon at five mosques in Riyadh two weeks during and two weeks following the insurrection, the religiosity of Al Saud and the moderate character of Islam were found to be the main themes. Prominent ulama appeared on television and radio programs emphasizing the compatibility between Islam and material well-being. In his weekly television program, Shaykh Ali al-Tentawi ridiculed

> the fanatics who lengthen their beards, refuse employment, devote their time to prayers and fasting, and pretend to be devout Muslims. This is not Islam [al-Tentawi noted]. This is an imitation of priesthood [al-rahbanah]. I myself enjoy material comfort, within my means, of course. I am married, work hard, and travel abroad. I also pray, fast, read the Quran regularly, and live according to the principles of the shari'ah. This is the sunnah of the prophet—to live your day as you will live for ever, and live for your tomorrow as if you will die today.[59]

To demonstrate its commitment to the enforcement of the *shari'ah*, the Saudi government reimposed the restrictions against females joining the work force, instructed foreigners to abide by the country's tradition and Islamic values, and closed down the video stores that were accused of renting or selling films that contradicted Islamic values and morals.

To gain ulama support, the government raised their salaries and allocated more funds to build mosques and to propagate Islam at home and abroad.[60] Funds were allocated to construct 241 mosques and to renovate 37 others.[61]

In the second policy Al Saud adopted following the insurrection, and in a clear move to pacify the secularists, a written Basic Law (*Nizam Asasi*) and Consultative Assembly were promised. On March 18, 1980, King Khalid ordered the creation of a committee to be headed by Prince Nayf, minister of the Interior, to "complete the drafting of the Basic Rules and a blueprint for a Consultative Assembly." The Saudi press was allowed to debate the issue. Consequently, a number of articles appeared that outlined the virtues of a written Basic Law and Consultative Assembly, showing that both were inherent in the Islamic political system.[62] Although such a Basic Law and Consultative Assembly were promised in Faisal's Ten Point Reform Program in 1962, they were not implemented. To date, they have not been introduced. Government reluctance to widen political participation may be viewed in terms of the king's dilemma: The widening of political participation will lead to Al Saud's loss of exclusive control; not to widen political participation will increase the emergent group's discontent and may lead to the loss of legitimacy.

Conclusion

The process of nation building initiated by Al Saud is reformist in nature; it attempted to satisfy simultaneously the needs of both the religious and the secular elements within the Saudi kingdom. Consistent with the regime's patrimonial character, Al Saud attempted to balance the interests and activities of both groups, but without affecting noticeable change in the political sphere.

Although female education was introduced, for example, its control remains under the ulama.

Al Saud reasserted Wahhabism as a state ideology while promoting material development. In the words of Ibn Saud, as directed to William Eddy, former U.S. ambassador to Saudi Arabia: "We Muslims have the one, true faith, but Allah gave you the iron which is inanimate, amoral, neither prohibited nor mentioned in the Quran. We will use your iron, but leave our faith alone."[63]

Can the "iron of the West" be introduced, however, without affecting the sociopolitical aspects of traditional society? The experience of Saudi Arabia has demonstrated that the process of nation building resulted in two developments beyond government control or desire. First, emergent groups began to demand political participation. Although Al Saud developed a complex bureaucracy, expanded the educational system, and initiated some development programs, politics remains the exclusive preserve of the royal family. By monopolizing political activity, and by proceeding with nation building, Al Saud have become prisoners of their own making: Nation building is necessary to survive domestically and externally, but the process of nation building will create groups that demand political participation. To share political authority with emergent groups means the erosion of patrimonial rule; not to share authority will intensify opposition and lead to the loss of legitimacy. Fortunately for Al Saud, the Saudi working class is small and not politicized, the intellectuals are a recent phenomenon and a weak one, and the military is supportive of the regime.

The second outcome of the process of nation building has been the erosion of traditional culture and relationships. Increased urbanization, literacy, the influx of migrant workers, the number of Saudis traveling abroad—all have contributed to the erosion of traditional culture. Eighteenth-century Wahhabism seems so antithetical to twentieth-century reality that many ulama have found themselves incapable of interpreting change or affecting its direction.

The continuous use of Wahhabi ideology without seriously modifying its content to suit reality has contributed to the weakening of the regime's legitimacy. The Mecca insurrection of 1979 was launched by a religious element that accused Al Saud of moral and religious laxity and advocated the revival of seventh-century Islamic government. Revivalist movements are often created to express their members' dissatisfaction with existing conditions and their desire for cultural regeneration. They are a "deliberate, organized, conscious effort by members of a society to construct a more satisfying culture."[64] The members of these movements perceive their existing culture, or some major areas of it, as unsatisfactory; thus they attempt to innovate or revitalize a new or old cultural system that they believe to be most appropriate for their condition.

The outcome of Al Saud's nation-building policy and the interaction between religion and state in the kingdom constitute a unique developmental experience—a quasi-capitalist mode of development in a semitribal traditional society; abundant financial resources and extreme affluence in a society governed by an austere and puritanical ideology; and a quasi-secular polity in which the ulama continue to influence national politics. The words of Imam al-Ghazali (1105 A.D.) may be an appropriate reminder to Al Saud that

> there is no hope in returning to a traditional faith after it has once been abandoned, since the essential condition in the holder of a traditional

faith is that he should not know that he is a traditionalist. Whenever he knows that, the glass of his traditional faith is broken. This is a breaking that cannot be mended, and a separation that cannot be united by any sewing or putting together, except it be melted in the fire and given another new form.[65]

7
Epilogue

Traditional Islamic political theory maintains that religion and state are indivisible. The purpose of government, therefore, is to preserve the *shari'ah* and enforce its dictates. God alone is sovereign and the source of all authority. Consequently, members of the *ummah* are God's subjects; the community's laws are divine; its property belongs to God; its army is God's army; and its opponents are the enemies of God. With these assumptions in mind, we have examined (1) the historical and theoretical development of the relationship between religion and state in Islam, and (2) the relationship between religion and state in the Kingdom of Saudi Arabia. The main concern was to search for answers to these ever-present questions: What is an Islamic state? What kind of relationship exists between the religious and political spheres in that state?

More than any other country in the Muslim world, Saudi Arabia is identified with Islam. In addition to the presence of Mecca and Medina, the center of Muslim prayers and pilgrimage, the kingdom's Islamic character was reconfirmed in 1745 when Shaykh Muhammad Ibn Abd al-Wahhab allied himself with Al Saud, the rulers of Dar'iya in central Najd. This alliance continues today. Islam is the state religion and its source of political legitimacy; it shapes educational and judicial activities and serves as the moral code of society. The observance of the traditional forms of Islam, as defined by the Wahhabis of eighteenth-century Arabia, remains an integral part of life. Business and government offices close for prayers; the *mutawi'a* make certain that Muslims attend public prayers and observe the moral code of Islam. Because of its fundamentalist ideology, and given the fact that the government supports a large number of Muslim organizations in addition to hosting more than 2,000,000 annual pilgrims in Mecca and Medina, the kingdom is viewed by Muslims as fundamentalist.

It has been noted by Shaykh Muhammad Ibn Abd al-Wahhab with respect to the ulama that because of their knowledge of Islamic laws their advice and their cooperation with the political authority are imperative. The ruler is responsible for the enforcement of religious obligations expected of Muslims—the fast, the pilgrimage, the application of *hudud* (punishments), the collection of zakat, and the commanding of good and forbidding of evil. The ulama are to advise their ruler and support him as long as he applies the word of God.

The relationship between Al Saud and the religious leaders in eighteenth-century Arabia was harmonious and corresponded closely to traditional Islamic political theory and to the principles outlined by Shaykh Muhammad Ibn Abd al-Wahhab. This harmonious relationship is surprising given that the study of the interaction between religion and state in Muslim history has demonstrated persistent conflict. The harmony in the first Saudi state may be attributed to the fact that both the religious and political spheres shared a complementarity of objectives. The existence of the first was dependent on the survival and continued support of the second. This alliance provided Muhammad Ibn Abd al-Wahhab with a political arm for his teachings and ensured Al Saud sanction from a recognized theologian as well as a body of converts capable of expanding his political authority and control of the Arabian Peninsula. Territorial expansion was justified in religious terms. More importantly, Wahhabi ideology served as a basis for the consolidation of Saudi rule. Obedience to the ruler was stressed as a religious duty. Since the ruler's function is to preserve and enforce the dictates of the *shari'ah*, rebellion against him was viewed as treason.

The findings of this study indicate that the state, because of its monopoly of force and resources and its need to maintain autonomy, cannot tolerate an autonomous religious domain that would compete with it for loyalty. The state will extend its authority to the religious domain and utilize religious leaders and institutions to perpetuate its policies. It will make use of religious values to strengthen its authority and legitimacy. But it will not hesitate to suppress religious institutions if they challenge its authority.

By maintaining the traditional alliance between his family and Al Shaykh, Ibn Saud projected his rule as a continuation of the first Saudi state. Ibn Saud identified the expansion of his rule with the expansion of Wahhabism. Although the ulama were generally supportive of his rule, aspiring to keep the ruler united to them through a common ideology, Ibn Saud's objective and policy shattered their hope. He needed Wahhabism to legitimate his authority, but innovation was also needed if the rule of Al Saud was to survive. Consequently, religion continued to be state ideology, the ulama were incorporated into state administration, and material development was introduced.

As Ibn Saud's experience with the Ikhwan demonstrated, the political sphere did not hesitate to suppress religious institutions when they challenged state authority. The Ikhwan demanded that their leader comply with the principles of Wahhabism. Their rebellion and its defeat in 1929 demonstrated the political sphere's determination to preserve its interests and, indeed, its very survival.

Following the Ikhwan's defeat and incorporation of the ulama into state administration, religion continued to constitute an important source of legitimacy. In their attempt to enhance governmental performance as a means of complementing the patrimonial base of the regime, and to control and direct the process of change that was precipitated by the discovery of oil, Al Saud established modern administrative institutions and initiated a nation-building program that included increased urbanization, literacy, and social services, as well as a higher standard of living.

The process of nation building led to two changes that affected the relationship between religion and state. First, it increased role differentiation between the religious and political spheres and routinized state control of a broad range of areas that were formerly controlled by religion. The outcome of this change was a relative secularization of the polity. Second, the initiation of nation-building policies resulted in events that fell beyond government control and affected the regime's patrimonial character.

Because of the religious heritage of the Saudi state and Al Saud's two-pronged policy of invoking religious legitimation of rule and justification of change while not allowing the religious establishment any measure of autonomy, secularization manifested itself through polity expansion. State jurisdiction now regulates societal areas that were formerly controlled by the religious sphere, and the ulama have become state administrators whose dogma and activities are supportive of the political leadership.

The initiation of nation-building policies led to outcomes that went beyond the wishes of the government. First, it produced new groups that challenged the regime's patrimonial character; second, it eroded traditional culture. Nation-building strategies were guided and influenced by the country's historical and cultural experience as well as by the interplay between reality and the aspiration of leadership. Al Saud adopted a reformist strategy that sought to maintain a viable socioeconomic order based on Wahhabism though flexible enough to adapt to changing conditions. Subsequently, while change was introduced to accommodate emergent needs, Wahhabism was invoked to rationalize change. Al Saud's reformist strategy created tensions in society that threatened the regime's survival. There were those who advocated rapid change, and also those, the fundamentalists, who demanded the preservation of the traditional order and ideology. Within each group, further tensions existed between supporters of Al Saud and those who advocated their ouster.

The supporters of Al Saud are for the most part secular-educated young Saudis, many of whom look to some of the younger and more liberal members of the royal family for guidance and support. This group advocates material change along with the maintenance of traditional values. They see no contradiction between Islam and material change. The size of this group is continuously increasing, and it plays an important role in shaping present Saudi politics. By contrast, a more radical younger generation of Saudis has emerged in recent years demanding the abolition of monarchical rule and the creation of a socialist order. This latter faction lacks leadership and a sense of direction. In addition, due both to the recent emergence of Saudi intellectuals as well as to their small size and government co-optation policy, this group does not pose an immediate threat to the survival of Al Saud.

A more immediate and serious threat to the stability of the regime is the fundamentalist faction. This faction includes state ulama and those fundamentalists who oppose both state ulama and Al Saud. Although the ulama benefit from Al Saud and support their rule, they attempt to control the public acceptance of innovations. They consider the expansion of secular education to be threatening to the Islamic character of the state. They aspire to preserve and enforce Wahhabi principles.

An even more radical fundamentalist faction also exists. This last group rejects all change and opposes Al Saud's rule. The most radical manifestation of its rejection of change as well as the authority of Al Saud is their seizure of the Grand Mosque in 1979. Their insurrection was defeated, but the dilemma confronting Al Saud remains unsolved— how to reconcile sudden and immense wealth, rapid modernization, and adherence to Wahhabi principles. Excluding external factors, the survival of the royal family depends on its ability to convert tensions into balances and to maintain control over the religious and secular elements, while at the same time modernizing the country to meet future challenges.

Notes

Chapter 1

1. Bernard Lewis, "Politics and War," in Joseph Schacht and C. E. Bosworth, eds., *The Legacy of Islam* (Oxford: Clarendon Press, 1974), p. 159.

2. Ibid., p. 160.

3. The Muhajerun were Muhammad's early followers who left Mecca with him in 622 A.D. to escape the consequences of embracing Islam. The Ansar were the Medinans who gave refuge to Muhammad and were credited for the initial success of Islam.

4. Lewis, "Politics and War," p. 160.

5. Yathrib is the pre-Islamic name of Medina. Muhammad's prophetic mission is divided into two periods. The first covers his life in Mecca, the city of his birth, from the time he began to receive the revelation to the day he left Mecca with some of his followers, fleeing from persecution. The second period covers his life in Medina. Muhammad's years in Medina are of importance to students of Islamic political theory because it was in that city that the first Islamic *ummah* was established and Islamic principles were implemented. Because Muhammad's emigration to Medina marks the foundation of the Muslim community, the Caliph Umar chose this year of *hijira* (emigration) to begin the Islamic calendar.

6. See Ahmad Ibn Hanbal, *al-Musnad*, vol. 3 (Beirut: Dar al-Nashr, n.d.), p. 152.

7. See Erwin I. J. Rosenthal, *Political Thought in Medieval Islam* (Cambridge, England: Cambridge University Press, 1962), pp. 61–62; and Lewis, "Politics and War," p. 159.

8. Cited in Abul A'la Maududi, "Political Thought in Early Islam," in M. M. Sharif, ed., *A History of Muslim Philosophy* vol. 1 (Wiesbaden: Otto Harrassowitz, 1963), p. 662.

9. Amir Hassan Siddiqui, "Islamic Institutions During the Pious Caliphate," *Voice of Islam* 10 (January 1961), pp. 188–189.

10. Muhammad al-Rayes, *al-Nazariyat al-Siyasiya al-Islamiya* (Cairo: al-Nasher, 1966), p. 42.

11. Bernard Lewis, *The Arabs in History* (New York: Harper & Row, 1960), p. 60.

12. On the verge of defeat, Mu'awiya called for arbitration, and Judge Abu Musa al-Asha'ari recommended that both contenders should step down, with the understanding that a new election would be held according to the principle of consultation. The result of the arbitration was bound to be in favor of Mu'awiya, who already possessed political power in Syria and had at his disposal sophisticated administrative machinery in Damascus. Ali's position was further weakened by divisions within his ranks. His supporters split into the Legitimists, the group that was later to develop into the Shi'i sect, and the Kharijites, who were angered by Ali's acceptance of arbitration and declared war on both contenders.

13. Lewis, "Politics and War," p. 166.

14. Ibid.

15. William Montgomery Watt, *Islamic Political Thought* (Edinburgh: Edinburgh University Press, 1968), p. 37.

16. See Nikki Keddie, ed., *Scholars, Saints, and Sufis* (Berkeley: University of California Press, 1978).

17. William Montgomery Watt, *The Majesty that Was Islam* (New York: Praeger Publishers, 1974), p. 109.

18. Bernard Lewis, *Islam and the Arab World* (New York: Alfred Knopf, 1977), p. 14.

19. Lewis, "Politics and War," p. 168.

20. Ibid., p. 172.

21. Sir Hamilton A. R. Gibb, "Constitutional Organization," in Majid Khadduri and Herbert Liebseney, eds., *Law in the Middle East* (Washington, D.C.: Middle East Institute, 1955), p. 6.

22. Lewis, "Politics and War," p. 163.

23. Ibid.

24. A.K.S. Lambton, "Islamic Political Thought," in Schacht and Bosworth, eds., *The Legacy of Islam*, p. 413.

25. G. E. Von Grunebaum, *Medieval Islam* (Chicago: Chicago University Press, 1946), p. 168.

26. See Wilfred Cantwell Smith, *Islam in Modern History* (Princeton, N.J.: Princeton University Press, 1957), especially Chapters 2 and 3.

27. On the role of al-Tahtawi in shaping the political mind of Egypt, see Jamal Muhammad Ahmad, *The Intellectual Origin of Egyptian Nationalism* (London: Oxford University Press, 1960).

28. See Anwar G. Chejne, "The Intellectual Revival in the Arab World: An Introduction," *Islamic Studies* 2 (December 1963).

29. Leon Zolondek, "al-Tahtawi and Political Freedom," *Muslim World* 59 (April 1964).

30. See Muhammad Abduh, *al-Islam Din al-Ilm wa al-Madaniya* (Cairo: Dar al-Hilal, n.d.).

31. Ali Abd al-Raziq, *al-Islam wa Usul al-Hukum* (Beirut: Dar al-Hayat, n.d.).

32. Khalid M. Khalid, *Min Huna Nabda'* (Cairo: al-Khangi Press, 1963).

33. Ibid., p. 47.

34. Khalid's radical statement concerning the separation of religion and state led to the confiscation of the book at the order of the censor of al-Azhar, who claimed that it constituted an "attack on the ecclesiastics and the capitalists in the traditional manner of the Communists." See Majid Fakhry, "The Theocratic Idea of the Islamic State in Recent Controversies," *International Affairs* 30, no. 4 (1954).

35. Donald Eugene Smith, ed., *Religion and Political Modernization* (New Haven, Conn.: Yale University Press, 1974), p. 6.

36. Stephen Humphreys, "Islam and Political Values in Saudi Arabia, Egypt and Syria," *Middle East Journal* 33, no. 1 (Winter 1979).

Chapter 2

1. S. N. Eisenstadt, "Religious Organizations and Political Process in Centralized Empires," *Journal of Asian Studies* 21, no. 3 (May 1962), p. 283.

2. Uthman Ibn Bishr, *Unwan al-Majd fi Tarikh Najd* (Riyadh: Maktabat Riyadh al-Haditha, n.d.), p. 6. Except when otherwise noted, the section on Muhammad Ibn Abd al-Wahhab and Wahhabi principles is based on Abd Allah al-Salih al-Uthaymin, *al-Shaykh Muhammad Ibn Abd al-Wahhab* (Riyadh: Dar al-Ulum, n.d.).

3. Wilfred Cantwell Smith, *Islam in Modern History* (Princeton, N.J.: Princeton University Press, 1957), p. 42. For a detailed and annotated bibliography on the Wahhabi movement, see Hisham Nashshabah, "Islam and Nationalism in the Arab world" (M.A. thesis, McGill University, Institute of Islamic Studies, 1955), pp. 7–26.

4. Ahmad Abd al-Ghafour Attar, *Muhammad Ibn Abd al-Wahhab* (Mecca: Mu'assasat Mecca li al-Nashr, 1979), p. 23.

5. Ibn Bishr, *Unwan al-Majd*, p. 7.

6. There is no mention by Najdi sources that Muhammad Ibn Abd al-Wahhab's travels extended beyond Najd, Hejaz, and Basra. Some authors claim that he visited Baghdad, Kurdistan, Hamadhan, Asfahan, Qum, Turkey, Aleppo, Damascus, Jerusalem, and Egypt. See, for example, *Lam' al-Shihab fi Sirat Muhammad Ibn Abd al-Wahhab*, by an unknown author, edited by Shaykh Abd al-Rahman Ibn Abd al-Latif Ibn Abd Allah al-Shaykh (Riyadh: Darat al-Malik Abd al-Aziz, 1974), pp. 3–17. For a contrary view, see Hamad al-Jasir, "Muarikhu Najd," *Majalat al-Jami'a* 3 (1959), pp. 39–49.

7. This book can be viewed as the manifesto of Wahhabi doctrine. It is divided into sixty-nine chapters, each of which advances *Quranic* verses and the *hadith* (traditions) of the Prophet to support the views of Muhammad Ibn Abd al-Wahhab. Following the *Quranic* verses and the *hadith*, quotations from the companions of the Prophet or their immediate successors are presented in support of the author's interpretation of these verses and traditions, and occasional references are made to later scholars such as Ibn Taymiya and Abu al-Qaym al-Jawziya. Finally, the author advances what he considers to be the appropriate conclusions to be drawn from his quotations.

8. Ibn Bishr, *Unwan al-Majd*, pp. 8–9.

9. Ibid.

10. Ibid., pp. 9–10. For refutation of Muhammad Ibn Abd al-Wahhab's views and activities, see Sayd Ahmad Ibn Zayni Dahlan, *al-Durar al-Saniya fi al-Rad ala al-Wahhabiya* (Cairo: Matba'at al-Bab al-Halabi, 1950). It must be noted at this point that the word *Wahhabism* was first used by the opponents of the movement but later on became an accepted term. The Wahhabis describe themselves as *muwahidin*, or unitarians. See Munir al-Ajlani, *al-Dawla al-Saudiya al-Ula* (Riyadh: n.p., n.d.), pp. 279–281.

11. *Dala'il al-Khayrat* was written by Muhammad al-Jazuli (d. 1441). This work, which praises the Prophet Muhammad, has been persistently recited in many parts of the Muslim world.

12. *Rawd al-Rayahin* was written by Abd Allah al-Yafi'i al-Yamani (d. 1366). It praises the Prophet Muhammad as well as his Companions.

13. Hussein Ibn Ghanam, *Tarikh Najd al-Musama Rawdat al-Afkar wa al-Afham li Murtad Hal al-Imam wa Ta'dud Ghawat Dha'i al-Islam* (Cairo: n.p., 1949).

14. Muhammad Ibn Abd al-Wahhab had criticized his own father, as well, for accepting fees from litigants. This criticism had strained the relations between the two.

15. Ibn Ghanam, *Tarikh Najd*, p. 32.

16. Ibn Bishr, *Unwan al-Majd*, pp. 10–11.

17. Ibn Ghanam, *Tarikh Najd*, p. 3.

18. Ibn Bishr, *Unwan al-Majd*, p. 12.

19. For a complete collection of the shaykh's letters to rulers, scholars, and tribal leaders in the Arabian Peninsula, see Muhammad Ibn Abd al-Wahhab, *Mu'alafat al-Shaykh al-Imam Muhammad Ibn Abd al-Wahhab*, vol. 5 (Riyadh: Imam Muhammad Ibn Saud Islamic University, n.d.).

20. Muhammad Ibn Abd al-Wahhab, *Kitab al-Tawhid* (Beirut: Holy Quran Publishing House, 1978), p. 14.

21. Cited in Shaykh Sulayman Ibn Abd Allah Ibn Muhammad Ibn Abd al-Wahhab, *Taysir al-Aziz al-Hamid fi Sharh Kitab al-Tawhid* (Riyadh: Directorate of Academic Research, Ifta', Propagation, and Guidance, n.d.), p. 17.

22. *The Quran*, Sura XX, Verse 110.

23. *The Quran*, Sura XX, Verse 5.

24. *The Quran*, Sura XX, Verse 6.

25. *The Quran*, Sura XVI, Verse 99.

26. Shaykh Sulayman Ibn Abd Allah, *Taysir al-Aziz*, p. 20.

27. For more information on the manner in which the Wahhabis view the Prophet, see Muhammad Ibn Abd al-Wahhab, *Sirat Rasul al-Lah* (vol. 3), in his collected works, *Mu'alafat al-Shaykh*.

28. Shaykh Sulayman Ibn Abd Allah, *Taysir al-Aziz*, p. 30.

29. Ibid., pp. 40–41.

30. Ibid., pp. 45–47.

31. The book of Shaykh Hamad Ibn Nasif Ibn Uthman Ibn Mu'amar (*Irshad al-Muslimin fi al-Rad ala al-Quburiyin* [Riyadh: Mu'assasat al-Nur, 1973]) argues the Wahhabi view on this issue.

32. Muhammad Ibn Abd al-Wahhab, *Kitab al-Tawhid*, pp. 42–43.

33. Ibid., pp. 43–44.

34. See the shaykh's letter to Ahmad Ibn Ibrahim, the *mutawi'* (enforcer) of the Murat area in al-Washim district, informing him of the need to attack the infidels and to confiscate their properties, in Muhammad Ibn Abd al-Wahhab, *Mu'alafat al-Shaykh*, vol. 5, pp. 204–210.

35. *The Quran*, Sura II, Verse 145.

36. Muhammad Ibn Abd al-Wahhab, *Mu'alafat al-Shaykh*, vol. 5, pp. 226–237.

37. See Muhammad Ibn Abd al-Wahhab, *Fadhl al-Islam* (vol. 1), in *Mu'alafat al-Shaykh*, pp. 225–227.

38. *The Quran*, Sura XXXIII, Verse 21.

39. Muhammad Ibn Abd al-Wahhab, *Mu'alafat al-Shaykh*, vol. 1, pp. 262–263.

40. In a letter sent to the Learned Men of Mecca, the shaykh rejected innovation by stating: "We are followers, not innovators." See Muhammad Ibn Abd al-Wahhab, *Mu'alafat al-Shaykh*, vol. 5, p. 40. In another letter sent to his followers, the shaykh wrote: "As for *ijtihad*, we are imitators of the Book, the Tradition, the Virtuous Ancestors and the Four Imams" (see ibid., p. 96).

41. A. D. Nock, *Conversion* (London: Oxford University Press, 1961), pp. 9–10.

42. Ibid.

43. See Muhammad Ibn Abd al-Wahhab, *Kitab al-Kaba'ir* (vol. 1), in *Mu'alafat al Shaykh*, pp. 45–46, in which the author devotes two chapters advising Muslims to obey their rulers and warning them against rebellion.

44. Qamaruddin Khan, *The Political Thought of Ibn Taymiyah* (Islamabad: Islamic Research Institute, 1973), p. 134.

45. Ibn Bishr, *Unwan al-Majd*, p. 15.

Part 2 Introduction

1. Reinhard Bendix, *Max Weber: An Intellectual Portrait* (New York: Anchor Books, 1962), p. 329.

2. Max Weber, *The Theory of Social Organization* (New York: Free Press, 1947), p. 358.

3. Bendix, *Max Weber*, p. 295.

4. Ibid.

5. Legitimacy is here defined as the citizen's conviction "that it is right and proper for him to accept and obey the authorities and to abide by the requirements of the regime." See David Easton, *A Systems Analysis of Political Life* (New York: Wiley, 1965), p. 278.

6. Bendix, *Max Weber*, pp. 296–297.

7. For a study of Ibn Saud's charismatic authority, see Bakr Omar Kashmeeri, "Ibn Saud: The Arabian Nation Builder" (Ph.D. dissertation, Howard University, Washington, D.C., 1973).

8. A third type is the feudal system, which was dominant in medieval European societies.

9. Bendix, *Max Weber,* pp. 330–331.

10. Ibid.

11. Ibid.

12. Manfred Halpern, "Four Contrasting Repertories of Human Relations in Islam," in L. Carl Brown and Norman Litzkowitz, eds., *Psychological Dimensions of Near Eastern Societies* (Princeton, N.J.: Darwin Press, 1977).

13. Ibid., p. 64.

14. James A. Bill and Carl Leiden, *Politics in the Middle East* (Boston: Little, Brown and Co., 1974), p. 152.

Chapter 3

1. The successful founding of a Saudi dominion in 1902 was presaged by two failed attempts. The first of these attempts followed the alliance that was forged between Al Saud and Al Shaykh, leading to the creation of the first Saudi state. However, the Saudi conquests of Mecca and Medina in 1803 and 1804, respectively, brought them into direct confrontation with the Ottoman sultan, who regarded himself as the Guardian of the Holy Places. Subsequently, the sultan requested Muhammad Ali, governor of Egypt, to put an end to Saudi control of the Holy Places. In 1812 Muhammad Ali's forces took Medina, and in the following year they took Mecca. In 1816 the Egyptians invaded Najd, and two years later the Saudi capital Dar'iya was razed to the ground. The second attempt to found a Saudi state occurred in 1824, when Turki Ibn Abd Allah Ibn Muhammad Al Saud seized Riyadh from Muhammad Ali's forces. The experiment ended in 1889. In that year, the Rashidis of Ha'il expelled Abd al-Rahman Ibn Abd Allah Al Saud from Riyadh. Abd al-Rahman and his family, including his son Ibn Saud, sought refuge in Kuwait. It was Ibn Saud, born around 1880, who reestablished his family's rule in Riyadh in 1902 and created the modern state of Saudi Arabia, thus initiating the third Saudi state.

2. For information on the relationship between Al Saud and the Rashidi family, see George Khairallah, *Arabia Reborn* (Albuquerque: University of New Mexico Press, 1953), p. 85.

3. Ibid.

4. Dankwart Rustow, ed., *Philosophers and Kings: Studies in Leadership* (New York: George Braziller, 1970), p. 26.

5. Ibid.

6. H. St. John Philby, *The Heart of Arabia,* vol. 1 (New York: G. P. Putnam's Sons, 1923), p. 297.

7. S. C. Snouck Hurgronje, *Mekka in the Latter Part of the 19th Century* (Leiden, Holland: E. J. Brill, 1931), pp. 190–203.

8. See Table 3.1.

9. Cited in Ahmad Abd al-Ghafur al-Attar, *Saqr al-Jazira* (Mecca: n.p., 1979), p. 572.

10. I. M. Lapidus, *Muslim Cities in the Later Middle Ages* (Cambridge, Mass.: Harvard University Press, 1967), p. 52.

11. H. C. Armstrong, *Lord of Arabia* (London: Arthur Barker Ltd., 1934), p. 214.

12. Hafiz Wahbah, "Wahhabism in Arabia: Past and Present," *Journal of Royal Central Asian Society* 16 (October 1924), p. 465.

13. Ahmed A. Shamekh, *Spatial Patterns of Bedouin Settlements in Al-Qasim Region, Saudi Arabia* (Lexington: University of Kentucky Press, 1975), pp. 46–47.

14. John Habib, *Ibn Saud's Warriors of Islam* (Leiden, Holland: E. J. Brill, 1978), p. 30.

15. *The Quran,* Sura IV, Verses 97–100.

16. Habib, *Ibn Saud's Warriors,* p. 111.

17. Ibid., p. 59.

18. Amin Rihani, *Ibn Sa'oud of Arabia* (Boston: Houghton Mifflin, 1928), p. 194.

19. It is necessary to note that among the bedouins a distinction is made between noble and ignoble tribes. The noble tribes are camel breeders, have a warrior tradition, and intermarry only with those of noble lineage. The ignoble tribes, by contrast, are semisedentary, do not have a warrior tradition, and perform menial work, which noble bedouins shun.

20. Rihani, *Ibn Sa'oud,* p. 194.

21. Habib, *Ibn Saud's Warriors,* p. 61.

22. Ibid.

23. Ibid., p. 63.

24. Ibid.

25. Hafiz Wahbah, *Jazirat al-Arab fi al-Qarn al-Ishrin* (Cairo: Maktabat al-Nahda al-Misriya, 1961), pp. 298–299.

26. Ibid.

27. For the full text of the ulama's *fatwa,* see *Um al-Qura* (February 12, 1927).

Chapter 4

1. For instance, in 1930 more than 70 percent of the students attending Dar al-Tawhid, a religious institution in Ta'if concerned with the teaching of the principles of Wahhabism as well as other Islamic sciences, were from Najd. The students received monthly stipends from the government, and upon graduation they were assigned administrative and religious positions.

2. *The Impact of Petroleum on the Economy of Saudi Arabia* (Riyadh: Ministry of Information, 1979), p. 4.

3. Kamal S. Sayegh, *Oil and Arab Regional Development* (New York: Praeger Publishers, 1968), pp. 81–82. The first concession to exploit Saudi oil was granted in 1933 to the Standard Oil Company of California, which in 1936 had sold a half-interest to the Texas Company and with which it was jointly renamed in 1944 the Arabian American Oil Company (ARAMCO). Four years later, the shareholdings in ARAMCO were redistributed among Standard of California (30 percent), Texas (30 percent), Standard of New Jersey (30

percent), and Socony Mobil (10 percent). In 1949 another concession was granted to the Pacific Western Oil Corporation (J. Paul Getty, 100 percent), covering all of Saudi Arabia's half-interest in the Saudi-Kuwait Neutral Zone. In 1950 the agreement with ARAMCO group was revised, increasing the Saudi share to 50 percent of the total profits. In 1957 Saudi Arabia granted a third concession to a Japanese company covering the offshore area of Saudi half-interest in the Neutral Zone, with Saudi Arabia receiving 56 percent of total profits, including those derived from refining, transportation, and marketing operations.

4. T. W. Schultz, "Economic Prospects of Primary Product," cited in ibid., p. 82.

5. Ibid.

6. For a study of the economic impact of the oil industry on Saudi society, see Fayez Bader, "Developmental Planning in Saudi Arabia: A Multi-Dimensional Study" (Ph.D. dissertation, University of Southern California, 1968).

7. Four and a half Saudi riyals are equal to one U.S. dollar. For information on state revenues, see *Annual Report 1978* (Riyadh: Saudi Arabian Monetary Agency, 1979).

8. H. St. John Philby, *Saudi Arabia* (Beirut: Librairie du Liban, 1968), p. xiii.

9. The text of the *fatwa* deposing King Saud is found in Hafiz Wahbah, *Arabian Days* (London: Arthur Barker Ltd., 1964), pp. 176–180.

10. James A. Bill and Carl Leiden, *Politics in the Middle East* (Boston: Little, Brown and Co., 1979), p. 155. Most of Ibn Saud's advisers were non-Saudis. Among them we can note Dr. Abd Allah Damluji from Iraq; Shaykh Yussef Yassin, Khalid Hakim, Dr. Mahmoud Hamdi Hamoudah, Dr. Midhat Shaykh al-Ard, Dr. Rashad Far'oun, and Khair al-Din al-Zirkli from Syria; Shaykh Fouad Hamzah from Lebanon; Shaykh Hafiz Wahbah from Egypt; and Khalid Kirkam from Libya.

11. There is also the Royal Court, which is divided into six administrative divisions—General Administration, Personnel, Translation, Press, Office of Bedouin Affairs, and Political Affairs. The Royal Court's activities, however, are limited to advising the king.

12. Mohammad Sadek, *Tatawur al-Nizam al-Siyassi wa al-Idari fi al-Mamlaka al-Arabiya al-Saudiya* (Riyadh: Ma'had al-Idara al-Ama, 1965), p. 28.

13. Ibid., p. 34.

14. Ibid., p. 36. See the royal decree ordering the establishment of the committee in *Umm al-Qura* [official gazette of Saudi Arabia and publisher of government documents], no. 186 (July 12, 1928).

15. See "Constitution of the Council of Ministers and Constitution of the Division of the Council of Ministers," *Umm al-Qura*, no. 1508 (March 1954).

16. Ibid., p. 7.

17. Ibid.

18. Ibrahim Muhammad al-Awaji, "Bureaucracy and Society in Saudi Arabia" (Ph.D. dissertation, University of Virginia, 1971), p. 127. For a study of the procedures and activities of the Saudi bureaucracy, see also Mohammad

A. Tawil, "The Procedures and Instruments of Administrative Development in Saudi Arabia" (Ph.D. dissertation, University of Pittsburgh, 1970).

19. For the Ministry of Finance and National Economy's organizational chart, see Fouad al-Farsy, *Saudi Arabia: A Case Study in Development* (London: Stacey International, 1978), p. 119.

20. Ibrahim al-Awaji, "Bureaucracy and Society," p. 128. For a study of the structure and function of these departments as well as those of the general public personnel administration, see Sulayman al-Mazyed, "The Structure and Function of Public Personnel Administration in Saudi Arabia" (Ph.D. dissertation, Claremont Men's College, Claremont, Calif., 1972).

21. al-Awaji, "Bureaucracy and Society."

22. Information on the Committees for Commanding the Good and Forbidding Evil was gathered through two interviews with the deputy director of the committees in Riyadh, March 11–12, 1980.

23. Shaykh al-Bitar's text was based on the writings of Taki al-Din Ahmad Ibn Taymiya, especially the work entitled *al-Hisba fi al-Islam* (Beirut: Dar al-Katib al-Arabi, n.d.).

24. Information on the directorate is compiled from an interview with the directorate's assistant director in Riyadh, October 10, 1979.

25. *Majmu'at al-Marasim al-Malakiya* (Riyadh: Government Printing Office, 1980), p. 81.

26. The present Higher Council of the Ifta' is composed of the following: Muhdar Afifi, Abd al-Razaq Afifi, Muhammad Amin al-Shanqiti, Abd Allah al-Khayat, Abd Allah Ibn Hamid, Abd al-Aziz Ibn Saleh, Abd al-Majid Hassan, Muhammad al-Harkan, Abd Allah al-Ghadyan, Muhammad Ibn Jubayr, Abd Allah Ibn Mani', Salih Ibn Luhaydan, Sulayman Ibn Ubaid, Ibrahim Ibn Muhammad Al Shaykh, and Rashid Ibn Hanyn.

27. Information was gathered from the Student Affairs Bureau at Riyadh University in 1979 and 1980.

28. al-Ma'had al-Islami, *Memorandum Submitted to the Islamic Secretariat for the Celebration of the Fourteenth Hijirah Century* (Riyadh: Islamic Institute, 1979), p. 8.

29. Information on WAMY was gathered in Riyadh, in 1979.

30. The 1977 conference, for example, was held in Kuala Lumpur and was attended by Muslim youth organizations from Afghanistan, Australia, Bangladesh, Fiji, Hong Kong, India, Indonesia, Japan, Malaysia, Pakistan, Singapore, Sri Lanka, South Korea, and Turkey.

31. For the director's views of the Islamic concept of international relations, see Abd al-Hamid Abu Sulayman, "The Islamic Theory of International Relations: Its Relevance, Past and Present" (Ph.D. dissertation, University of Pennsylvania, 1973).

32. A representative sample of the books includes Muhammad Qutub, *Shubuhat Hawl al-Islam* (al-Itihad al-Islami, n.p., n.d.); Abd al-Qadir Awda, *al-Islam wa Awda'una al-Qanuniya* (Damascus: Holy Koran Publishing House, 1977); and Sayid Qutub, *al-Mustakbal li hadha al-Din* (Damascus: Holy Koran Publishing House, 1978).

33. Muhammad Qutub, *Shubuhat*, p. xi.

34. Richard H. Nolte, "The Rule of Law in the Arab Middle East," *Muslim World* 48 (October 1958), pp. 295–296.

35. Subhi al-Mahmasani, *al-Awda' al-Tashri'iya wa al-Qada'iha fi al-Bilad al-Arabiya* (Beirut: Dar al-Ilm li al-Malayin, 1965), pp. 443–464.

36. Ibid.

37. The Arabic text of the *fatwa* is found in Hafiz Wahba, *Jazirat al-Arab* (Cairo: n.p., n.d.), pp. 319–321.

38. *Majmu'at al-Nuzum fi Qism al-Qada' al-Shar'i* (Mecca: *Umm al-Qura*, 1938), p. 8.

39. *Umm al-Qura* (August 5, 1927).

40. *Umm al-Qura* (March 24, 1934).

41. *Umm al-Qura* (June 7, 1926).

42. Ibid.

43. The order noted the following: first, that citizens can mail their complaints to the Royal Court; second, that grievances can be brought directly to the Royal Court; third, that the complainant may request an audience with the king for an oral presentation of his grievance; and fourth, that a complainant can wait and present his grievance to the king outside the royal palace.

44. *Majmu'at al-Nuzum*, pp. 9–12.

45. Soliman Solaim, "Constitutional and Judicial Organization in Saudi Arabia" (Ph.D. dissertation, Johns Hopkins University, 1970), p. 94.

46. Ibid.

47. Ibid., p. 132.

48. The texts are as follows: Musa al-Hijawi, *al-Igna';* Mansur al-Hanbali al-Buhuti, *Kashf al-Qina' an Matn al-Igna';* al-Futuhi, *Muntaha al-Iradat;* Mansur al-Buhuti, *Sharh Muntaha al-Iradat;* Shams al-Din al-Qudamah, *al-Mughni;* and Abd al-Rahman Ibn Qudamah, *al-Sharh al-Kabir.*

49. See Sa'dun al-Jasir, *al-Shari'ah fi al-Mamlaka al-Arabiya al-Saudiya* (Riyadh: Ma'had al-Da'wa al-Islami, 1973).

50. Quoted in Abd al-Karim al-Huqayl, *Alagat al-Muwatin bi al-Dawa'ir al-Shari'iya* (Beirut: Dar al-Ma'arif, 1967), pp. 189–190.

Chapter 5

1. James Bill, "The Patterns of Elite Politics in Iran," in George Lenczwoski, ed., *Political Elites in the Middle East* (Washington, D.C.: American Enterprise Institute, 1975), p. 17.

2. For information on the number of graduates from Saudi religious and secular universities between 1945 and 1970, see William Rugh, "Emergence of a New Middle Class in Saudi Arabia," *Middle East Journal* 27, no. 1 (Winter 1973).

3. Ibid., p. 12.

4. Ibid.

5. For an excellent article on the educational background, career pattern, and social outlook of al-Tariki, see Stephen Duguid, "A Biographical Approach to the Study of Social Change in the Middle East: Abdallah Tariki as a New Man," *International Journal of Middle East Studies* 1, no. 3 (1970).

6. See Norman C. Walpole et al., *Area Handbook for Saudi Arabia* (Washington, D.C.: Government Printing Office, 1965), p. 157. For a description of the genealogical evolution of Al Saud, see Fouad al-Farsy, *Saudi Arabia: A Case Study in Development* (London: Stacey International, 1978), pp. 63–66.

7. David Howarth, *The Desert King* (Beirut: Continental Publications, n.d.), p. 110.

8. H. C. Armstrong, *Lord of Arabia* (London: Arthur Barker Ltd., 1934), p. 175.

9. Information on the royal family was gathered through interviews during field research in 1979 and 1980.

10. Rodger P. Davis, "Syrian Arabic Kinship Terms," *Southwestern Journal of Anthropology* 5 (Autumn 1949), p. 249.

11. For an examination of the changing character of the Saudi tribal society, see Motoko Katakura, *Bedouin Village: A Study of a Saudi Arabian People in Transition* (Tokyo: University of Tokyo Press, 1977).

12. Information on King Faisal's children was gathered during field research in 1979 and 1980, from *Who's Who in Saudi Arabia, 1977* (London: Europa Publications, 1978), and *ARAMCO World Magazine* 30, no. 3 (May-June, 1979).

13. William Rugh, "Emergence of a New Middle Class," p. 12.

14. Biographic information is derived and compiled from *Who's Who in Saudi Arabia 1976–1977* (Jeddah: Tihama, 1978); from *al-Dara* (Riyadh: Darat al-Malik Abd al-Aziz); and through interviews during my field research in Saudi Arabia in 1979–1980. Information on ministers from the royal family is dealt with in Table 5.2.

15. *The Second Five Year Plan* (Riyadh: Ministry of Planning, 1975), p. 1.

16. See Ahmad Zaki al-Yamani, *Islamic Law and Contemporary Issues* (Karachi: Elite Publishers, 1958), pp. 9–10.

17. The survey was conducted in 1970 by Ibrahim al-Awaji, the current deputy minister of the interior. It included interviews with 271 key civil servants. The sample represents about 9 percent of a population of 3,000 civil servants in grades 2 to 4, who work for 19 central state organizations in Riyadh. See Ibrahim Muhammad al-Awaji, "Bureaucracy and Society in Saudi Arabia" (Ph.D. dissertation, University of Virginia, 1971).

18. Ibid., p. 192.

19. Ibid., pp. 228–229.

20. Ibid., p. 188.

21. Ibid.

22. See, for example, Fred W. Riggs, *Administration in Developing Countries: The Theory of Prismatic Society* (Boston: Houghton Mifflin, 1964), and, by the same author, "An Ecological Approach: The 'Sala' Model," in Ferrel Heady, ed., *Papers in Comparative Public Administration* (Ann Arbor: University of Michigan Press, Institute of Public Administration, 1962).

Chapter 6

1. Samuel P. Huntington, *Political Order in Changing Societies* (New Haven, Conn.: Yale University Press, 1968), p. 177.

2. Manfred Halpern, *The Politics of Social Change in the Middle East and North Africa* (Princeton, N.J.: Princeton University Press, 1963), p. 10.

3. For information on the events leading to Faisal's assumption of power and its consequences, see Richard H. Nolte, "Faisal Takes Over in Saudi Arabia," *Reporter* 18 (May 1958); "A Saudi Revolution," *Economist* (April 30, 1960); and "al-Tatawur fi Ahd al-Malik Faisal," *al-Bilad* (April 23, 1971). Saud's ouster reflected the royal family's concern with survival and its willingness to adapt to changing circumstances. This concern was voiced by a family member to a Lebanese journalist: "The royal family had been faced with the alternatives either of allowing the monarchy to disintegrate or of bringing the conflict [between Faisal and Saud] to an end. We preferred to sacrifice Saud rather than the country." Cited in Gerald deGaury, *Faisal, King of Saudi Arabia* (New York: Praeger Publishers, 1966), p. 134.

4. Cited in Norman C. Walpole et al., *Area Handbook for Saudi Arabia* (Washington, D.C.: Government Printing Office, 1966), pp. 156–157.

5. See George Lenczowski, "Saudi Arabia: Tradition and Reform," in George Lenczowski, ed., *The Political Awakening in the Middle East* (Englewood Cliffs, N.J.: Prentice-Hall, 1970), p. 171; and Fouad al-Farsy, "King Faisal's Concept of Saudi Arabian Development," *Majalat al-Talib* 1, no. 2 (Riyadh University, Hijirah, fourteenth ["Islamic Hijira"] century).

6. UNESCO, Office of Statistics, *Educational Studies and Documents* 4, no. 53 (1965), p. 16.

7. See *Statistical Yearbook, 1968* (Riyadh: Department of Central Statistics, 1969), p. 117; and *The Middle East and North Africa, 1975–1976* (London: Europa Publications, 1975), p. 605.

8. *Statistical Yearbook, 1980* (Riyadh: Ministry of Planning, 1980), pp. 88–89.

9. Ibid.

10. Government of Saudi Arabia, *The Educational Policy in The Kingdom of Saudi Arabia,* article 153 (Riyadh: Ministry of Education, n.d.).

11. *Outline of the Second Five Year Plan* (Riyadh: Ministry of Information, 1980), p. 1.

12. This information was gathered from interviews with Saudi educators during field research in 1979 and 1980.

13. *al-Jazirah* (June 7, 1980). For information on the number and fields of Saudis studying abroad, see "al-ibti'ath al-Khariji," in ibid.

14. *Akhbar al-Mub'taith,* no. 12 (Hijirah, fourteenth century).

15. *Umm al-Qura* (October 23, 1959).

16. Government of Saudi Arabia, *The Educational Policy in the Kingdom of Saudi Arabia,* p. 33.

17. Saad Eddin Ibrahim, *The New Arab Social Order* (Boulder, Colo.: Westview Press, 1982), p. 95.

18. *al-Jazirah,* no. 2880 (June 18, 1980).

19. Ibrahim, *The New Arab Social Order,* p. 105. For information on the tremendous expansion of the construction industry in Saudi Arabia, see ARAMCO, *A Directory of Construction Contractors in the Kingdom of Saudi Arabia* (Dhahran: Local Industrial Development Department, 1980); ARAMCO, *The Central Region Construction Industry* (Dhahran: Local Industrial Development Department, 1978); and ARAMCO, *The Saudi Arabian Market for Bulk Construction Materials* (Dhahran: Local Industrial Development Department, 1979).

20. These objectives are pursued by a strategy that calls for (1) acceleration of the growth rate of the gross domestic product (GDP), (2) manpower development, and (3) diversification of sources of income to reduce the economy's dependence on oil by increasing the contribution of non-oil domestic production. The development policy is based on the goals of (1) free enterprise and trade, (2) a balanced budget, and (3) an emergency reserve of foreign exchange sufficient to maintain the country's imports for two years. To implement these goals, government expenditures are caused to flow in three directions: (1) to finance physical and social infra-structures, (2) to extend financial assistance to private enterprises and private consumers, and (3) to build the country's holding of foreign exchange and assets. For information on government economic objectives, see *Outline of the Second Five Year Plan* (Riyadh: Ministry of Information, 1980), and A. M. Sharshar, "Oil, Religion, and Mercantilism: A Case Study of Saudi Arabia's Economic System," *Studies in Comparative International Development* 12, no. 3 (Fall 1977). It must be noted that oil is the major contributor to government revenues. This sector contributed 60 percent of the GDP and 90 percent of government revenues in 1972. Information on Saudi economic development is derived from an interview with William Hostetler at ARAMCO (Local Industrial Development Department, Dhahran, February 20, 1980).

21. Imports rose from over $3 billion in 1974 to $17 billion in 1978–1979.

22. Ibrahim, *The New Arab Social Order,* p. 107.

23. For information on the role and status of Saudi women, see Catherine Parssinen, "The Changing Role of Women," in Willard Beling, ed., *King Faisal and the Modernization of Saudi Arabia* (Boulder, Colo.: Westview Press, 1980); and Fatina Shaker, "The Status of Women in Islam and Their Changing Role in Saudi Arabia" (M.A. thesis, Texas Woman's University, 1966).

24. In some Gulf states (e.g., Qatar, Kuwait, and the United Arab Emirates), expatriates outnumber the native population. See "Labor Migration in the Middle East," *MERIP Reports,* no. 59 (1977); and Ibrahim, *The New Arab Social Order.*

25. Ibrahim, *The New Arab Social Order.*

26. For a description of the law, see George Lenczowski, *Oil and State in the Middle East* (Ithaca, New York: Cornell University Press, 1960), p. 258.

27. Lenczowski, *Oil and State,* p. 272.

28. John A. Shaw and David E. Long, *Saudi Arabian Modernization* (Washington, D.C.: Georgetown University, Center for Strategic and International Studies, 1982), pp. 66–67.

29. Ibid.

30. *Gazette* (October 15, 1980).

31. Information on opposition within the military is derived from *Saut al-Tali'a* 2, no. 6 (June 1974), and *Political Opposition in Saudi Arabia* (San Francisco: *Saut al-Tali'ah,* 1980).

32. *Afro-Asian Affairs* (November 9, 1977).

33. Edward Shils, "The Intellectuals in the Political Development of the New States," in Jason L. Finkle and Richard W. Gable, eds., *Political Development and Social Change* (New York: John Wiley & Sons, 1971), p. 250.

34. Ibid., p. 251.

35. Cited in Helen Lackner, *A House Built on Sand: A Political Economy of Saudi Arabia* (London: Ithaca Press, 1978), p. 104.

36. *MERIP Reports,* no. 91 (October 1980).

37. Among the literature we can note *Pillars of the Saudi Monarchy; Saudi Justice, the Execution of a Prince's Political Opposition in Saudi Arabia; The Neo-Ikhwan Seize the Grand Mosque in Mecca "Saudi Arabia"*

38. *Tariq al-Sha'b* (September 26, 1977). See also *Political Opposition in Saudi Arabia* (San Francisco: *Saut al-Tali'a,* 1980).

39. Organization of the Islamic Revolution, *The Word of People* (n.p., n.d.).

40. Information on the insurrection was gathered from Riyadh Radio broadcasts, which were monitored during the seizure, from the Saudi press, and from interviews with two Saudis who claim to have known Juhaiman.

41. The first reference to the number of rebels was made by Saud al-Faisal, who noted that "from the information we have so far, the number of men inside the mosque does not exceed 200. They are of various nationalities, and lightly armed" (*al-Jazirah* [November 22, 1979]). Shaykh Muhammad Ibn Sabeel, Imam of the Mosque, estimated the number as falling between 300 and 400 (*al-Bilad* [November 24, 1979]). Major Muhammad al-Nufai'ey, a spokesman for the Ministry of Defense, placed their number between 300 and 500 (*al-Jazirah* [November 28, 1979]). Prince Nayf countered this last estimate by noting that "from the information we have . . . their number is 200, or maybe a little more" (*al-Jazirah* [November 28, 1979]).

42. *al-Nahar* reported that the ten Egyptians were members of the *takfir wa hijrah* group (*al-Nahar* [January 10, 1980]). The sixty-three insurgents were executed in eight Saudi cities on January 9, 1980. For the names and nationalities of all sixty-three, see *al-Jazirah* (January 9, 1980).

43. This information was taken from an interview with two imams at the Grand Mosque in Mecca on February 10, 1980.

44. Ibid.

45. David Holden and Richard Johns, *The House of Saud* (New York: Holt, Rinehart & Winston, 1981), p. 521.

46. Ibid.

47. In a press conference, Prince Nayf noted that between 1977 and 1979 the following number of arms were confiscated from smugglers:

- 7,258 handguns with 720,575 rounds of ammunition
- 1,127 rifles with 126,489 rounds of ammunition
- 1,060 hunting rifles with 137,120 rounds of ammunition

- 363 small hunting weapons with 600 rounds of ammunition
- 481 machine guns with 337,034 rounds of ammunition

For further details, see *al-Jazirah* (January 10, 1980).
48. *Thawra fi Rihab Makkah* (San Francisco: *Saut al-Tali'a*, 1980), pp. 105–123.
49. The insurrection took place as Muslims were celebrating the beginning of the fifteenth Islamic century. The Mahdi was proclaimed at the Ka'ba.
50. *Da'wat al-Ikhwan, Kayfa Bada'at wa Ila Ayna Tasir* (n.p., n.d.). The following pamphlets are attributed to Juhaiman:

1. *Al Imara wa al-Bayia wa Kashf Talbis al-Hukam ala talabat al Ilm wa al-Awam*, 37 pages
2. *Da'wat al-Ikhwan, Kayfa Bada'at wa Ila Aya-Tasir*, 36 pages
3. *al-Mizan li-Hayat al-Insan*, 27 pages
4. *Mukhtasar al-Hasana li-Ibn Taymiyah*, 29 pages
5. *Raf' al-Iltibas An Milat man Ja'lahu al-Lah Imam al-Nas*, 20 pages
6. *Mukhtasar al-Amr bi al-Ma'rouf wa al-Nahi an al-Munkar*, 34 pages
7. *al-Fitan wa Akhbar al-Mahdi al-Dajal*, 30 pages
8. *al-Fitra al-Salima*, 10 pages

51. *al-Jazirah* (November 22, 1979).
52. *al-Hawadith* (January 18, 1980).
53. *al-Safir* (January 9, 1980).
54. See Muhammad Ibn Abd al-Wahhab, *Mu'alafat al-Shaykh al-Imam Muhammad Ibn Abd al-Wahhab*, vol. 5 (Riyadh: Ibn Muhammad Ibn Saud Islamic University, n.d.), pp. 234–245.
55. For the full text of the *fatwa*, see *al-Sharq al-Awsat* (November 26, 1979). The *fatwa* was signed by thirty prominent ulama. See also *Journal of Muslim World League*, no. 7 (January 1980).
56. Women and children were put under state custody to be "taught orthodox Islam." See *al-Siyassa* (December 13, 1979).
57. This interview was conducted in Riyadh on March 5, 1980.
58. Riyadh Television, May 19, 1980. Shaykh Ali al-Tentawi, who is Syrian by origin, went on self-exile to Saudi Arabia in 1963 following the coming to power of the Baath party in Syria.
59. In an effort to defuse the protest against the non-Muslim expatriates in the kingdom, the Saudi press published reports showing the expatriates' respect of Islam. For example, *al-Jazirah* noted on December 12, 1979, that Korean workers are highly respectful of Islam: "Some workers were seen stopping work during the call to prayers in reverence to Islam."
60. *al-Yom* (April 12, 1980).
61. *al-Jazirah* (March 22, 1980).
62. William A. Eddy, "King Ibn Saud: Our Faith and Your Iron," *Middle East Journal* 17, no. 3 (Summer 1963), p. 257.
63. Anthony F. C. Wallace, "Revitalization Movements," *American Anthropologist* 57, no. 58 (April 1956), p. 265. For an excellent bibliographic study of these movements, see Weston La Barre, "Materials for a History of Studies

of Crisis Cults: A Bibliographic Essay," *Current Anthropology* 12, no. 1 (February 1971), and Johannes Fabian, "The Anthropology of Religious Movements: From Explanation to Interpretation," *Social Research* 46 (1979).

64. Cited in Manfred Halpern, *The Politics of Social Change in the Middle East and North Africa* (Princeton, N.J.: Princeton University Press, 1963), p. 31.

Selected Bibliography

Books

Abdo, Albert N. *Saudi Arabia.* Washington, D.C.: Department of Commerce, 1962.

Armstrong, H. C. *Lord of Arabia.* London: Arthur Barker Ltd., 1934.

Arnold, Sir Thomas W. *The Caliphate.* Oxford: Clarendon Press, 1924.

Asad, Mohammad. *The Road to Mecca.* New York: Simon and Schuster, 1954.

————. *The Principles of State and Government in Islam.* Los Angeles: University of California Press, 1961.

Beling, Willard A., ed. *King Faisal and the Modernization of Saudi Arabia.* Boulder, Colo.: Westview Press, 1980.

Bendix, Reinhard. *Max Weber: An Intellectual Portrait.* New York: Anchor Books, 1962.

————. *Nation Building and Citizenship.* New York: Doubleday and Co., 1969.

Benoist-Mechin, Jacques. *Arabian Destiny.* New York: Essential Books, 1958.

Berger, Morroe. *The Arab World Today.* New York: Doubleday and Co, 1962.

Berkes, Niyazi. *The Development of Secularism in Turkey.* Montreal: McGill University Press, 1964.

Bill, James A., and Carl Leiden. *Politics in the Middle East.* Boston: Little, Brown and Co., 1979.

Black, C. E. *The Dynamics of Modernization.* New York: Harper & Row, 1966.

Butler, Grant C. *King and Camels: An American in Saudi Arabia.* New York: Devin-Adair Co., 1961.

Caroe, Olaf. *Wells of Power.* New York: Macmillan Publishing Co., 1951.

Champinois, Lucien, and Jean-Louis Soulie. *Le Royaume d'Arabie Saoudite Face à l'Islam Révolutionnaire.* Paris: Cahiers de la Fondation Nationale de Sciences Politiques, 1966.

Cheney, Michael. *Big Oil Man from Arabia.* New York: Ballantine Books, 1958.

Deutsch, Karl, and William Foltz. *Nation Building.* New York: Atherton Press, 1963.

Dodge, Bayard. "The Significance of Religion in Arab Nationalism," in Harris J. Proctor, ed., *Islam and International Relations.* New York: Doubleday and Co., 1965.

Doughty, Charles M. *Travels in Arabia Deserta.* New York: Random House, 1936.

al-Farsy, Fouad. *Saudi Arabia: A Case Study in Development.* London: Stacey International, 1978.

deGaury, Gerald. *Rulers of Mecca.* London: George C. Harrap and Co., 1951.

———. *Faisal, King of Saudi Arabia.* New York: Praeger Publishers, 1966.

Gerth, H., and C. W. Mills, eds. *From Max Weber.* New York: Oxford University Press, 1972.

Glubb, Sir John. *War in the Desert.* New York: W. W. Norton & Co., 1961.

Habib, John. *Ibn Saud's Warriors of Islam.* Leiden, Holland: E. J. Brill, 1978.

Halpern, Manfred. *The Politics of Social Change in the Middle East and North Africa.* Princeton, N.J.: Princeton University Press, 1963.

Hamilton, Charles Walter. *Americans and Oil in the Middle East.* Houston, Tex.: Gulf Publishing Co., 1962.

Hazard, Hary W. *Saudi Arabia.* New Haven, Conn.: Hraf Press, 1956.

Holden, David, and Richard Johns. *The House of Saud.* New York: Holt, Rinehart & Winston, 1981.

Howarth, David. *The Desert King.* Beirut: Continental Publications, n.d.

Huntington, Samuel P. *Political Order in Changing Societies.* New Haven, Conn.: Yale University Press, 1968.

Ibrahim, Saad Eddin. *The New Arab Social Order.* Boulder, Colo.: Westview Press, 1982.

Johnstone, Ronald L. *Religion and Society in Interaction.* Englewood Cliffs, N.J.: Prentice-Hall, 1975.

Jowitt, Kenneth. *Revolutionary Breakthroughs and National Development.* Berkeley: University of California Press, 1964.

Keddie, Nikki, ed. *Scholars, Saints, and Sufis.* Berkeley: University of California Press, 1978.

Khadduri, Majid. "From Religious to National Law," in Jack Thompson and Robert Reischauer, eds., *Modernization of the Arab World.* Princeton, N.J.: Van Nostrand, 1966.

Lackner, Helen. *A House Built on Sand: A Political Economy of Saudi Arabia.* London: Ithaca Press, 1978.

Lebkicher, Roy. *The Arabia of Ibn Saud.* New York: Russell F. Moore Co., 1952.

Lenczowski, George. *Oil and State in the Middle East.* Ithaca, N.Y.: Cornell University Press, 1960.

Lenczowski, George, ed. *The Political Awakening in the Middle East.* Englewood Cliffs, N.J.: Prentice-Hall, 1970.

———. *Political Elites in the Middle East.* Washington, D.C.: American Enterprise Institute, 1975.

Lerner, Daniel. *The Passing of the Traditional Society.* New York: Free Press, 1967.

Levy, Reuben. *The Social Structure of Islam.* Cambridge: Cambridge University Press, 1962.

Lewis, Bernard. "Politics and War," in Joseph Schacht and C. E. Bosworth, eds., *The Legacy of Islam.* Oxford: Clarendon Press, 1974.

Lipsky, George. *Saudi Arabia.* New Haven, Conn.: Hraf Press, 1959.

Longrigg, S. H. *Oil in the Middle East.* New York: Oxford University Press, 1954.

Nock, A. D. *Conversion.* London: Oxford University Press, 1961.

O'Dea, Thomas. *The Sociology of Religion.* Englewood Cliffs, N.J.: Prentice-Hall, 1966.

Philby, John. *Arabia of the Wahhabis.* London: Constable and Co., 1928.

_____. *The Empty Quarter.* London: Constable and Co., 1933.

_____. *Arabian Days.* London: Hale, 1948.

_____. *Arabian Highlands.* Ithaca, N.Y.: Cornell University Press, 1952.

_____. *Arabian Jubilee.* London: Hale, 1952.

_____. *Saudi Arabia.* London: Ernest Benn Ltd., 1955.

_____. *Forty Years in the Wilderness.* London: Hale, 1957.

Rihani, Amin. *Ibn Sa'oud of Arabia.* Boston: Houghton Mifflin, 1928.

Roosevelt, Kermit. *Arabs, Oil and History.* New York: Harper Brothers, 1949.

Sadek, Mohammad. *The Development of Government Administration in Saudi Arabia.* Riyadh: Institute of Public Administration, 1965.

Sayegh, Kamal S. *Oil and Arab Regional Development.* New York: Praeger Publishers, 1968.

Shamekh, Ahmed A. *Spatial Patterns of Bedouin Settlements in Al-Qasim Region, Saudi Arabia.* Lexington: University of Kentucky Press, 1975.

Shaw, John A., and David E. Long. *Saudi Arabian Modernization.* Washington, D.C.: Georgetown University, Center for Strategic and International Studies, 1982.

Smith, Donald Eugene. *Religion and Political Development.* Boston: Little, Brown and Co., 1970.

_____. *Religion and Political Modernization.* New Haven, Conn.: Yale University Press, 1974.

Smith, Wilfred Cantwell. *Islam in Modern History.* Princeton, N.J.: Princeton University Press, 1957.

Wahbah, Hafiz. *Arabian Days.* London: Arthur Barker Ltd., 1964.

Williams, Kenneth. *Ibn Saud.* London: Jonathon Cape, 1933.

Winder, Richard B. *Saudi Arabia in the Nineteenth Century.* London: Macmillan Publishers, 1965.

Yinger, Milton J. *Religion, Society and the Individual.* New York: Macmillan Publishing Co., 1957.

_____. *The Scientific Study of Religion.* New York: Macmillan Publishing Co., 1970.

Articles

Amine, Ahmad. "Ijtihad in Islam." *Islamic Review* 39, no. 12 (1951).

Barthwick, M. "The Islamic Sermon as a Channel of Political Communication." *Middle East Journal* 21 (Summer 1967).

Coulson, N. J. "Doctrine and Practice in Islamic Law." *Bulletin of the School of Oriental and African Studies* 18 (1956).

Duguid, Stephen. "A Biographical Approach to the Study of Social Change in the Middle East: Abdallah Tariki as a New Man." *International Journal of Middle East Studies* 1, no. 3 (1970).

Eddy, William A. "King Ibn Saud: Our Faith and Your Iron." *Middle East Journal* 17, no. 3 (Summer 1963).

Edens, David G., and William P. Snavely. "Planning for Economic Development in Saudi Arabia." *Middle East Journal* 24, no. 1 (Winter 1970).

Eisenstadt, S. N. "Religious Organizations and Political Process in Centralized Empires." *Journal of Asian Studies* 21, no. 3 (May 1962).

al-Farsy, Fouad. "King Faisal's Concept of Saudi Arabian Development." *Majalat al-Talib* 1, no. 2 (Riyadh University, Hejirah, fourteenth century).

Gibb, H.A.R. "Al-Mawardi's Theory of the Caliphate." *Islamic Culture* 2 (July 1937).

––––––. "Some Considerations on the Sunni Theory of the Caliphate." *Archives d'Historic du Droit Oriental* 2 (1948).

––––––. "The Evolution of Government in Early Islam." *Studia Islamica* 4 (1955).

Harrington, Charles W. "The Saudi Arabian Council of Ministers." *Middle East Journal* 17 (Summer 1958).

Hart, Parker T. "Application of Hanbalite and Decree Law to Foreigners in Saudi Arabia." *George Washington Law Review* 22 (December 1953).

al-Husayni, Musa. "The Institution of the Hisbah in Early Islam: Or a study of Ethical Standards Expected of Islamic Society." *Islamic Review* 57 (February 1969).

Khadduri, Majid. "The Judicial Theory of the Islamic State." *Muslim World* 41 (July 1951).

Kohn, Hans. "The Unification of Arabia." *Foreign Affairs* 13 (October 1934).

Laitin, David. "Religion and Political Culture and the Weberian Tradition." *World Politics* 30 (July 1978).

Mahmassani, Sobhi. "Muslims' Decadence and Renaissance: Adaptation of Islamic Jurisprudence to Modern Social Needs." *Muslim World* 44 (1954).

Malone, Joseph J. "Saudi Arabia." *Muslim World* 56 (October 1966).

Phily, H. J. "The New Reign in Saudi Arabia." *Foreign Affairs* 32 (April 1954).

Rentz, George. "Saudi Arabia: The Islamic Island." *Journal of International Affairs* 19 (1965).

Rosenthal, Erwin. "Some Reflections on the Separation of Religion and Politics in Modern Islam." *Islamic Studies* 3 (September 1964).

Rugh, William. "Emergence of a New Middle Class in Saudi Arabia." *Middle East Journal* 27 (Winter 1973).

Saab, Hasan. "The Spirit of Reform in Islam." *Islamic Studies* 2 (March 1966).

Sanger, Richard. "Ibn Saud's Program for Arabia." *Middle East Journal* 1 (1947).

Shamma, Samir. "Law and Lawyers in Saudi Arabia." *International and Comparative Law Quarterly* 14 (July 1965).

Sharabi, Hisham. "The Crisis of the Intelligentsia in the Middle East." *The Muslim World* 47 (July 1957).

Sheean, Vincent. "King Faisal's First Year." *Foreign Affairs* 44 (January 1966).
Siegman, Henry. "The State and the Individual in Sunni Islam." *Muslim World* 54 (January 1964).
Sullivan, Robert R. "Saudi Arabia in International Politics." *Review of Politics* (October 1970).
Tannous, Afif. "The Arab Tribal Community in a Nationalist State." *Middle East Journal* 1 (1947).
Wahbah, Hafiz. "Wahhabism in Arabia Past and Present." *Journal of the Central Asian Society* 16 (1929).
_____ . "What Actually is Wahhabism?" *Islamic Review* 37 (December 1949).
Watt, D. C. "The Foreign Policy of Ibn Saud." *Royal Central Asian Society* (April 1963).

Theses and Dissertations

al-Awaji, Ibrahim Muhammad. "Bureaucracy and Society in Saudi Arabia." Ph.D. dissertation, University of Virginia, 1971.
al-Erris, Tarik. "Saudi Arabia: A Study in Nation Building." Ph.D. dissertation, American University (Washington, D.C.), 1968.
Goldrup, Lawrence Paul. "Saudi Arabia: 1902–1932: The Development of a Wahhabi Society." Ph.D. dissertation, University of California, 1971.
al-Gosaibi, Khalid. "A Study of the Industrial and Agricultural Potentialities of Saudi Arabia." M.A. thesis, University of Southern California, 1964.
al-Hamad, Sadun. "The Legislative Process and the Development of Saudi Arabia." Ph.D. dissertation, University of Southern California, 1973.
al-Mazyed, Sulayman. "The Structure and Function of Public Personnel Administration in Saudi Arabia." Ph.D. dissertation, Claremont Men's College (Claremont, Calif.), 1972.
Shaker, Fatina. "The Status of Women in Islam and Their Changing Role in Saudi Arabia." M.A. thesis, Texas Woman's University, 1966.
_____ . "Modernization of Developing Nations: Saudi Arabia." Ph.D. dissertation, Purdue University, 1972.
Solaim, Soliman. "Constitutional and Judicial Organization in Saudi Arabia." Ph.D. dissertation, Johns Hopkins University, 1970.
Tawil, Mohammad A. "The Procedures and Instruments of Administrative Development in Saudi Arabia." Ph.D. dissertation, University of Pittsburgh, 1970.
al-Yami, Ali Hassan. "The Impact of Modernization on the Stability of the Saudi Monarchy." Ph.D. dissertation, Claremont Graduate School (Claremont, Calif.), 1972.

Arabic Readings

The following is a list of Arabic literature on Saudi Arabia. The list contains four sections: (1) Saudi government publications, (2) articles in Saudi academic journals, (3) Saudi daily and weekly journals, and (4) books on Saudi Arabia.

مراجع باللغة العربية

١ ـ وثائق حكومية

ـ نظام الشركات ، مكة ، مطبعة الحكومة ، ١٩٦٨

ـ نظام كتاب العدل، مكه، مطبعة الحكومة ، ١٩٦٧

ـ نظام تركيز مسؤوليات القطاع الشرعي ، مطبعة الحكومة ، ١٩٦٢

ـ نظام تأديب الموظفين ، مكه ، مطبعة الحكومة ، ١٩٧١

ـ نظام مجلس الوزراء ، مكه ، مطبعة الحكومة ، ١٩٦٥

ـ نظام محاكمة الوزراء ، مكه ، مطبعة الحكومة ، ١٩٦٤

ـ نظام العمل والعمال ، مكه ، مطبعة الحكومة ، ١٩٦١

ـ تنظيم الاعمال الادارية في الدوائر الحكومية ، مطبعة الحكومة ، ١٩٦٣

ـ مجموعة النظم ، مطبعة ام القرى ، ١٩٣٩

ـ تعليمات تميز الاحكام الشرعية ، الرياض ، معهد الادارة العامة ، ١٩٦٦

ـ نظام الوكالات التجارية ، مكه ، مطبعة الحكومة ، ١٩٦٣

ـ نظام الضمان الاجتماعي ، مكه ، مطبعة الحكومة ، ١٩٦٣

ـ النظام التجارى ، مكه ، مطبعة الحكومة ، ١٩٤٩

ـ نظام مكافحة الغش التجارى ، مطبعة الحكومة ، مكه ، ١٩٦٣

ـ الخطة الخمسية الثانية ، وزارة الاعلام

ـ الخطة الخمسية الثالثة ، وزارة الاعلام

٢ ــ مقالات

ــ صالح الحسين ، " تعليق حول امكانيات القضاء الاداري في الدولة الاسلامية "
مجلة الادارة العامة ، كانون الثاني ، ١٩٦٤ .

ــ سعد العلام ، " القضاء الاداري في المملكة   مجلة الادارة العامة ، اذار،١٩٦٥ .

ــ محمد صادق ، " تنظيم الاعمال الادارية في الدوائر الشرعية " ، مجلة الادارة ،
١٩٦٦ .

٣ ــ مجلات علمية وجرائد يومية ومجلات اسبوعية

ــ السفير

ــ الحوادث

ــ ام القرى

ــ الجزيرة

ــ الرياض

ــ اليوم

ــ مجلة الادارة العامة

ــ الطليعة

ــ الشرق الاوسط

ــ الداره

ــ المجتمع

ــ الدعوه

ــ مجلة النفط

ــ اليمامه

٤ ــ الكتب

ــ ابراهيم فصيح بن السُيد صبغة الله الحيدرى ، عنوان المجد في بيان احوال
بغداد وبصره ونجد ، بغداد ، دار البصرى ، دون تاريخ .

ــ احمد السباعي ، تاريخ مكه ، دراسات في السياسة والعلم والاجتماع ،
القاهرة ، دار الكاتب ، ١٩٤٨ .

ــ ابراهيم جمعة ، الاطلس التاريخي للدولة السعودية ، الرياض ، دارة الملك
عبد العزيز ، ١٩٧٧ .

ــ احمد بن زيني دحلان ، خلاصة الكلام في بيان امراء البلد الحرام ،
القاهرة ، بدون تاريخ .

ــ حسن سليمان محمود ، تاريخ المملكة العربية السعودية ، القاهرة ، ١٩٦٦ .

ــ حسين بن غنام ، روضة الافكار والافهام لمرتاد حالة الامام وتعداد غزوات
ذوى الاسلام ، القاهرة ، ١٩٦٠ .

ــ سليمان بن عبدالله بن محمد بن عبد الوهاب ، كتاب التوضيح عن توحيـــد
الخلاق في جواب اهل العراق وتذكرة اولى   الباب في طريقة محمد بن عبدالوهاب
القاهرة ، ١٩٠١ .

ــ ـــــــــــــــــ ، تيسير العزيز الحميد في شرح كتاب التوحيد
رياض ، دار العلوم ، بدون تاريخ .

ــ سليمان بن عبد الوهاب ، الصواعق الالهية في الرد على الوهابية ،
القاهرة ، بدون تاريخ .

ــ عبد الحميد بطريق ، الوهابيه دين ودولـه ، بحث منشور في حولية كلية البنـات في جامعة عين شمس ، ١٩٦٤ .

ــ عبد الرحيم عبد الرحمن عبد الرحيم ، الدولة السعودية الاولى ، القاهـــــرة دار الكتاب الجامعي ، ١٩٧٩ .

ــ عثمان بن بشر ، عنوان المجد في تاريخ نجد ، مكه المكرمه ، ١٩٣٠

ــ عبد السلام حسن عبد الهادى ، تطور الادارة العامة في المملكة العربية السعودية الرياض ، دار المعارف السعودية ، ١٩٧٨ .

ــ علي عبد الرزاق ، الاسلام واصول الحكم ، بيروت ، بدون تاريخ .

ــ عبد العزيز بن محمد المرشد ، نظام الحسبه في الاسلام ، الرياض ، معهد القضاء العالي ، ١٩٧٣ .

ــ عبد العزيز سيد الاهل ، داعية التوحيد ، بيروت ، دار العلم للملايين ، بدون تاريخ .

ــ احمد عبد الغفور العطار ، محمد بن عبد الوهاب ، مكه ، موءسسة مكتبة النشر ١٩٧٩ .

ــ عبد الرحمن ابن عبد اللطيف ابن عبدالله ابن عبد اللطيف الشيخ ، علمـاء الدعوة ، القاهرة ، مطبعة الميداني ، ١٩٦٦ .

ــ محمد بن عبد الوهاب ، موءلفات الشيخ الامام محمد بن عبد الوهاب ١٢ جزء الرياض ، جامعة الامام محمد ابن سعود الاسلامية ، بدون تاريخ .

ــ فريد مصطفى ، ال سعود ، دمشق ، بدون تاريخ .

ــ قدرى قلعجى ، موعد مع الشجاعة ، الرياض ، دار النشر ، بدون تاريخ .

ــ مجموعة الرسائل والمسائل النجدية ، القاهرة ، المطبعة السلفيه ، بدون تاريخ .

ــ محمد حامد الفقي ، اثر الحركة الوهابية في الحياة الاجتماعية والعمرانية
القاهرة ، ١٩٣٥ .

ــ محمد رشيد رضا ، الوهابيون والحجاز ، القاهرة ، ١٩٢٥ .

Index